services marketing communications products

USEFUL IDEAS FROM JAPAN

283 USEFUL IDEAS FROM JAPAN

by Leonard Koren

illustration by Shack Mihara

research by Ziggie Kato

Chronicle Books • San Francisco

Printed in Japan.

Library of Congress
Cataloging in Publication Data

Koren, Leonard.
283 useful ideas from Japan / Leonard
Koren.
p.   cm.
ISBN 0-87701-483-3 (pbk.)
1. Commercial products—Japan.
2. Service industries—Japan.
3. Marketing—Japan.
4. Communications—Japan.
I. Title.
HF1040.9.J3K67 1988
338'.02'0952—dc19   88-1093
                            CIP

Distributed in Canada
by Raincoast Books
112 East Third Avenue
Vancouver, B.C.
V5T 1C8

10 9 8 7 6 5 4 3 2 1

Chronicle Books
San Francisco, California

CONTENTS

Introduction 10

products CAPSULE OFFICE BUILDING 14

products TEMPORARY AND SEMIPERMEABLE SIDEWALKS 15

products URINE AND HOT OIL SOLIDIFIERS 16

products STYLISH FIVE- AND SIX-DOOR REFRIGERATORS 17

products NEW FOOD CONCOCTIONS 18

products DESIGNER FRUIT 20

products HEAD-COOLING PILLOWS 21

products TWO-HEADED PUBLIC TELEPHONE 22

products ANTI–OBSCENE-PHONE-CALL MACHINE 23

products SING-ALONG MACHINES 24

products COZY TABLE/DESK 25

products SENSOR-CONTROLLED MIRRORS 26

products HOME DOUBLE-DECKER GARAGE 27

products AUTOMATED PREFAB DOWNTOWN PARKING TOWER 28

products RETRACTABLE CARWASH 30

products WASHING MACHINE CLEANING ENHANCERS 31

products CREATIVE HOUSEWARES 32

products COMBINATION TOILET-SINK 34

products TOILET FOR HEMORRHOID SUFFERERS 35

products ACCESSORIES FOR THE JAPANESE BATH 36

products HOT SPRINGS WATER DELIVERY SERVICE 37

products INSTANT REJUVENATION AIDS 38

products BELLY BANDS, FACE MASKS, AND STRESS GUM 39

products A FEW MORE ZANY IDEAS 40

services FULL-SERVICE TAXIS 44

services HOUSEHOLD MOVING SERVICES 46

services DRIVE-HOME SERVICE 48

services AIRPORT AND DEPARTMENT STORE COURTESY STAFF 49

services ELIMINATING BANK LINES 50

services LAND TRUSTS 51

services HANDYMAN AGENCIES 52

services HAIRSTYLE PRE-IMAGING AND SCALP MASSAGES 53

services FOOD SERVICE AMENITIES 54

CONTENTS

services   HOME FOOD DELIVERY IN REAL DISHES   55

services   COFFEE SHOP CONCEPTS   56

services   TINY BARS   58

services   BOTTLE KEEP AND ENDLESS APPETIZERS   59

services   CAPSULE HOTELS   60

services   COIN SNEAKER LAUNDRY   62

services   SAFETY-BOX UNDERWEAR LAUNDRY   63

services   COMMUNITY PUBLIC BATHS   64

services   PAPER-RECYCLING TRUCK   66

services   TELEPHONE SERVICES FOR BUSY PEOPLE   67

services   COSMETIC SURGERY TO IMPROVE YOUR LIFE   68

services   AUTOMOBILE BODY CLONING   69

marketing   BAR CONCEPTS   72

marketing   RESTAURANT PROMOTIONS   73

marketing   SADISTIC CUISINES   74

marketing   CATCH-AS-CATCH-CAN CUISINE   75

marketing   ONE INGREDIENT, MULTICOURSE RESTAURANTS   76

marketing   COOK-IT-YOURSELF RESTAURANTS   77

marketing   RENTAL RESTAURANTS   78

marketing   ROOFTOP BEER GARDENS   79

marketing   RESTAURANTS ON WHEELS   80

marketing   THEME TRAIN CARS   81

marketing   STORES BENEATH TRAINS AND ROADBEDS   82

marketing   VENDING MACHINES   84

marketing   CROSS MERCHANDISING   86

marketing   FOOD AND CROP FUTURES   87

marketing   INDEPENDENT KINGDOMS   88

marketing   SELECTED-ITEM CONSUMER DAYS   90

marketing   CONVENIENT FOODSTUFF PACKAGING   91

marketing   NOVELTY LIQUOR, BEER, AND SAKE PACKAGING   92

marketing   PACKAGING OF EVERYDAY PRODUCTS   94

marketing   COORDINATED STATIONERY SYSTEMS   96

marketing   GENERIC MERCHANDISE STORE   97

marketing   PREPAID DESIGNER TELEPHONE CARDS   98

marketing   ALL-ORACLE BUILDING   100

CONTENTS

marketing   COUNTRY BUMPKIN TOURS   101

marketing   LOVE HOTELS   102

marketing   THEME WEDDINGS   104

marketing   THEME PARK CONCEPTS   106

marketing   HOT SPRINGS ATTRACTIONS   108

marketing   JAPANESE INNS   110

marketing   ULTRA-PERSISTENT VIDEO HARD SELL   112

marketing   DEPARTMENT STORE MERCHANDISING TIPS   114

marketing   CONCEPT BUILDINGS   116

communications   CHANGE MACHINES AND REAL-TIME MAPS   120

communications   PUBLIC POLLUTION MONITORS   121

communications   BUILDING CONVENTIONS   122

communications   VIDEO BILLBOARDS ON WHEELS   123

communications   UNIQUE TV SHOWS   124

communications   EFFECTIVE TV COMMERCIALS   126

communications   BUS AND SUBWAY ADVERTISING   127

communications   TISSUE PAPER GIVEAWAYS   128

communications   TRANSFERABLE DEBT PAYMENTS   129

communications   CORPORATE COMIC BOOKS   130

communications   MAGAZINE AND COMIC BOOK CONCEPTS   132

communications   UNIQUE BOOK CONCEPTS   134

communications   TEACHING BASIC VALUES   136

communications   PREVENTING AUTO ACCIDENTS   137

communications   POLICE BOXES   138

communications   "NO SHOES INDOORS" SYSTEM   139

communications   TELEPHONE AIDS FOR THE DISABLED   140

communications   MAKING CITIES SAFER FOR THE BLIND   141

communications   MESSAGE AND INFORMATION CENTERS   142

communications   MAGAZINE HOUSE   144

communications   PUBLIC GATHERING PLACES   146

communications   TAKING CORPORATE RESPONSIBILITY   147

communications   SUGGESTION BOXES   148

communications   ENCOURAGING EMPLOYEE CREATIVITY   149

Appendix   152

Thanks   174

INTRODUCTION

If you've spent time abroad you've probably seen some product or service during your travels and thought, "Why don't they have that in my country?" Maybe what you saw was a different kind of telephone. Maybe it was a potato peeler. Maybe it was a way of handling customers or providing information. Whatever it was, you knew it was a great idea, and that if you could just remember it long enough to get it home there was probably some way you could use it to start your own business or give your existing business the competitive edge it needs.

Here for armchair entrepreneurs is a collection of useful business ideas from Japan. Why Japan? Because Japan is a country that "does things better," or so many people think. Because Japan, an Asian nation, brings fresh assumptions and methods to a weary Western industrialized world. And because Japanese consumer concepts—via Japanese consumer goods and investments—are swiftly becoming American consumer concepts. The Japanese are survivors. They are the world's retailers par excellence. They are ferociously competitive. Yet nowhere else is found such a high regard for total customer satisfaction and the bedrock virtues of quality and service. Maybe these are things our own country has to learn again.

The ideas are divided into four groupings: products, services, marketing, and communications. This grouping is somewhat arbitrary, since many ideas transcend any one category. There are over a hundred separate topics, but within each topic there may be several related ideas. Since *283 Useful Ideas* was the working title of this book we decided to stay with that number. In fact there are many more.

The use of comic book–style illustrations in a business book was deliberate. Pictures get ideas across with a lot less explanation. They encourage the kinds of associations and visualizations that are the stuff of creativity. Also, the drawings—by a Japanese illustrator in Tokyo—bring out many important cultural inflections that can't be adequately expressed in words. The drawings are accompanied by brief captions. Prices are given in yen, because that's what you'll pay in Japan and because currency rates fluctuate too wildly to make dollar amounts meaningful (but for a rough approximation, figure ¥130 = $1). An appendix at the back of the book expands on most of the captions and tells which manufacturers and people to contact for further information. One useful idea to pass on here is that, when in Japan, don't just call up companies and expect to talk business. Do it the Japanese way: Find someone who speaks Japanese and work through a knowledgeable intermediary.

Finally, this book offers some very useful ideas about Japan and the Japanese. Seeing the tools, devices, and systems that a culture uses, we can't help but piece together a portrait of that culture. We see Japanese cultural preoccupations, specialities, beliefs, deficiencies. A secondary aspect of this book therefore is to provide insights into the way Japanese people—whose future is enormously important to our own—think and live.

CAPSULE OFFICE BUILDING

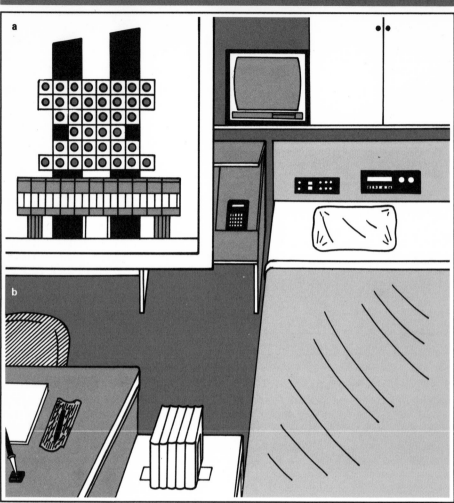

a   The Nakagin Capsule Tower Building in the Ginza is made up of 140 cantilevered boxes. The modular approach allows the building to change shape over time according to use. Each capsule measures eight by thirteen feet (the maximum size allowed on highways) and can also be used singly as an extra room in a garden or as a mobile home.

b   A machine for living. Three-capsule units were originally sold as condos and came with bed, cupboards, TV, fridge, wardrobe, storage space, desk, telephone, sound equipment, bathroom, and good soundproofing. Most are owned by out-of-town companies as Tokyo *pieds-à-terre*.

TEMPORARY AND SEMIPERMEABLE SIDEWALKS

- New underground cables, sewer pipes, temporary construction access, road widening: It seems like our streets and sidewalks are always being torn up. Tokyo crews now use standard modular concrete curb elements that are easy and fast to install, thus reducing the cost and inconvenience of roadwork. City planners are also trying out a semipermeable sidewalk material that allows water to soak into the ground instead of running into the sewers and being lost. By raising the water table they hope to restore some of the city's natural geologic balance as well as to mitigate the damage from a major earthquake.

URINE AND HOT OIL SOLIDIFIERS

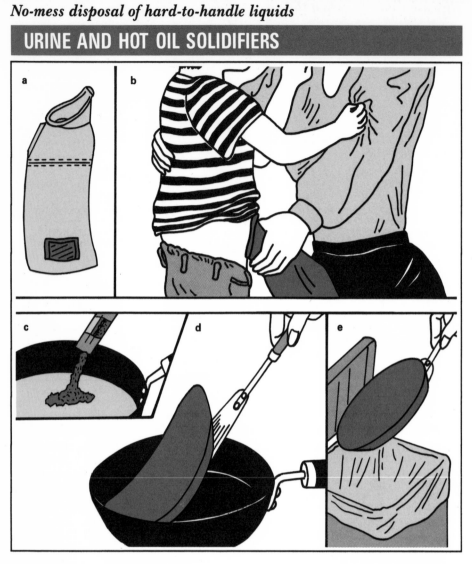

a   The Urea Pot, a disposable porta-potty. Fits both sexes.

b   The product comes in handy when in a car with kids or on a boat with no toilet. It is also convenient for the bedridden and the elderly. After use, add the chemical in the attached side-pouch; in a few seconds the urine turns into an environmentally safe gel you later flush away or dispose of in a nearby garbage pail.

c/e For used cooking oil, use Katameru Tempuru ("Get Solid!"). This vegetable product contains no chemical additives and comes five packs to a box for ¥295. Mix into hot oil; as the mixture cools it becomes solid for disposal with regular garbage.

STYLISH FIVE- AND SIX-DOOR REFRIGERATORS

- Isolated compartments within a refrigerator let you custom fit the cooling environment to different kinds of food. These Japanese models are computer controlled and artfully designed to look like furniture. One comes with a built-in microwave oven and an odor-remover. Some compartments are (1) quick freezer, which freezes three to four times faster than conventional freezers; (2) "partial" freezer, which keeps meat and fish just above freezing, allowing maximum storage and flavor retention with no defrosting; (3) "chilled" zone, for regular foods; (4) vegetable area, which adjusts moisture level.

NEW FOOD CONCOCTIONS

- A lack of Western food prejudices has led the Japanese to create some wondrous new flavor combinations. For example:

a   Ice creams (*left to right*): sweet potato, oolong tea, blue cheese, *wasabi* (horseradish), tomato & lemon, black sesame seed, red bean, and basil leaf are just a few of the flavors available at Tokyo ice cream parlors.

b   Joan Restaurant in Tokyo's Shinjuku district serves *udon* (thick white wheat noodles) with chocolate sauce and almonds. Elsewhere you can get noodles garnished with perfectly digestible flakes of gold leaf (at roughly four times the cost of regular noodles).

c *Soba* sushi: raw fish on beds of tied and twisted buckwheat noodles.

d Curry-flavored bagels, a bit smaller than the American variety. Another crowd pleaser is "jelly" donuts filled with curry sauce, fish sausage, or red bean paste. Sandwiches worth sampling can be made of spaghetti or breaded, deep-fried potato patties on hot dog rolls. Then there's chocolate bread.

e Hot cocoa with 2 percent chili sauce.

f Canned drinks offered in vending machines. Café au lait is sold hot or cold, and oolong tea comes with and without milk. Green tea is available in plastic containers with attached drinking spouts.

Edible "objets": look good, taste good

DESIGNER FRUIT

a

b

c

a Melons with neatly trimmed stems are sold in cardboard and wooden gift boxes. Cost ranges ¥2,500 to ¥10,000 depending on quality. The fruit is grown hanging in the air from strings to ensure a perfect sphere and picked at the precise moment of ripeness. Japanese think of these as gifts, not as "food."

b Watermelons can be grown inside a container to any rectangular or pyramidal shape you order.

c Farmers take orders for apples with a personal message "grown into" the skin. These are often used at weddings. Inscribing is done with a masking material that grows with the apple.

HEAD-COOLING PILLOWS

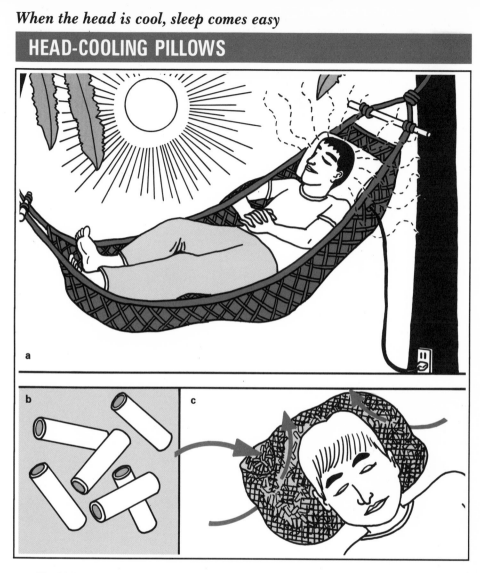

a   The high-tech solution: Keeping the head cool on hot summer nights makes going to sleep easier. Plug in the pillow an hour before bedtime, and it will cool down to 16° F below body temperature. The deluxe model has a designer cover, an on-off light, a strong-weak switch, and a timer. Costs only 50 cents a month to run on regular house current.

b/c   The low-tech solution: Fill a fine mesh pillow case with these hollow polyethylene cylinders, about one inch long by a half-inch wide. Your weight causes the cylinders to adjust exactly to the shape of your head and allow air to circulate and cool as you sleep.

TWO-HEADED PUBLIC TELEPHONE

- You and a friend are in the city and want to meet another friend for dinner. But where? Call her up and the three of you can discuss it together on a public telephone with two receivers. One person listens as the other takes down directions. Money-making tip: These dual handset units tend to encourage 20 to 30 percent longer conversations. The sixty that have been installed in Japan since summer 1986 have long lines of people waiting to use them. All new Japanese phone booths—single-receiver booths, too—come with mirrors attached so that telephoners can groom themselves after calling ahead to announce they are on their way.

ANTI–OBSCENE-PHONE-CALL MACHINE

a   How do you deal with unwanted phone calls, including heavy breathers and telephone marketers? Change your number? No. Sony's Telephone Keyboard answering machine offers prerecorded fight-back messages. Access any message by selecting a key when you pick up the phone. Press one key and a threatening male voice yells out, "What the ——— do *you* want?!" Press another key and the ear of the offending party gets shot with a blast of 100 decibels. Costs ¥17,000.

b   The Revenge Telephone (also by Sony) uses an integrated circuit to repeat an obscene message at a caller for as long as he is on the line.

SING-ALONG MACHINES

a   *Karaoke* ("empty orchestra") is Japan's national pastime of singing in bars to machine-supplied musical accompaniment. Cassette and laser disk players generously enhance amateur voices with professional effects like echoes. One model has a computer to check whether you're on key and digitally displays your score on a scale of 1 to 100. Some models have prerecorded voice tracks that come on automatically when you forget the lyrics.

b   A laser disk plays music and video to enhance the mood. Pioneer's "Love Fantasy" comes in two formats, landscape scenery and porno story, for public and intimate showings.

COZY TABLE/DESK

- Many Japanese homes lacking central heating use a *kotatsu* in winter. This low, square table has a mild heat source below and a quilt or blanket on top to trap the warm air. You put your legs under the table to keep them warm while your head stays cool and alert. A *kotatsu* saves money on heating and becomes the focal point of family life in winter—a modern hearth. Traditionally, the *kotatsu* was a pit with coals. Today, an electronic heating element is usually attached to the underside of the table. A flat top placed on the blanket makes the *kotatsu* useful for eating, games, or writing. In summer, the blanket is removed.

SENSOR-CONTROLLED MIRRORS

- In densely populated areas sunlight is at a premium. A sophisticated mirror system called Natulight, used in shopping centers, department stores, and residences to funnel in sunlight, makes interior spaces more comfortable and appealing. Sensors cause the mirrors to rotate as the sun moves across the sky. The mirrors have a high-reflection finish so that 70 to 90 percent of the light is saved. As an option you can control the amount of ultraviolet and infrared to help regulate heating in summer and winter. At night and when it's raining, the sensors shut down to save money. A home system costs ¥1.5– 3 million, plus 20 percent to install.

HOME DOUBLE-DECKER GARAGE

- In some areas in Japan, a person cannot buy a car unless he has a place to park it. Here, then, is an idea for people who need their yard space as well as a place to put their second car. Called the Rittai Garage ("Three Dimensional Garage"), this clever home parking center costs ¥2.35 million plus installation. It is ten feet wide and twenty feet high. Regular maintenance is available for a fee. The top car must go in before the second car is brought in, and vice versa. However, since the roof completely obscures the car on top, valuable classic or rarely driven cars can be stored without anyone realizing they're there.

27

AUTOMATED PREFAB DOWNTOWN PARKING TOWER

a

a   Street parking is almost nonexistent in Japanese cities, and little land is available for new garages. At the same time, more and more Japanese own cars. One solution to this growing problem uses narrow and difficult sites as locations for prefab steel-frame parking towers. These towers, when freestanding, have concrete or fireproof-slat exteriors that blend into the surrounding urban landscape, making them look much like office buildings. They can also be built into existing buildings. Inside, a computer-controlled conveyor and storage system—much like a ferris wheel—packs away anywhere from ten to fifty cars, two abreast, depend-

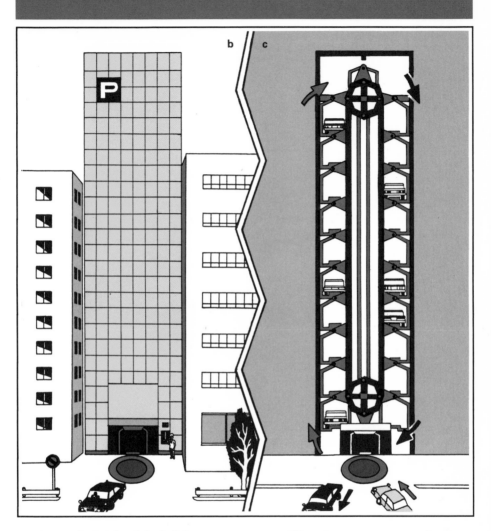

ing on the height of the building. Parking towers can be purchased for ¥40–80 million, not including the cost of the land.

b   Enter the tower at street level. The ferris-wheel elevator presents an empty slot at the entryway and, after the customer has gotten out, lifts the car into the tower.

c   When the customer returns he presents his claim ticket and waits for the car to come down from the tower. If he has not backed into the tower to begin with, when he leaves he can back out onto a round metal platform that will turn the car around so that it can be driven straight out into traffic.

For small gas stations and parking garages

RETRACTABLE CARWASH

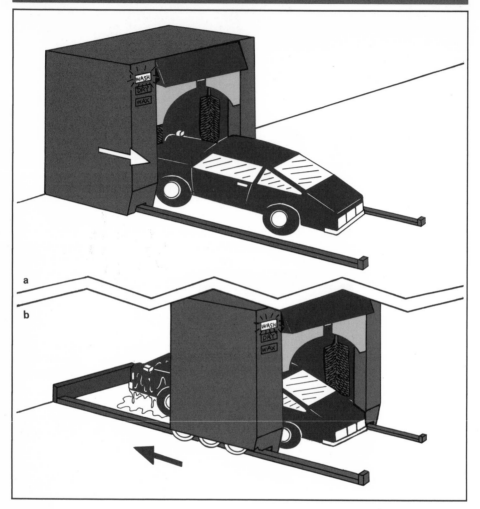

a   Park your car between the tracks at the mouth of the carwash. Select from eight different computerized wash and wax sequences. The hood moves across your car in two-minute cycles. The most elaborate wash job takes only eight minutes.

b   A gas station owner can buy this carwash, including installation, for about ¥5 million. It comes complete with sponges and brushes and a liquid dispersal unit. One popular marketing technique is to sell regular customers monthly passes allowing unlimited use for about ¥5,000. The entire carwash, which takes up only 360 square feet, fits perfectly in a small corner of a city gas station.

Micro-turbulence and flotation action get clothes cleaner

WASHING MACHINE CLEANING ENHANCERS

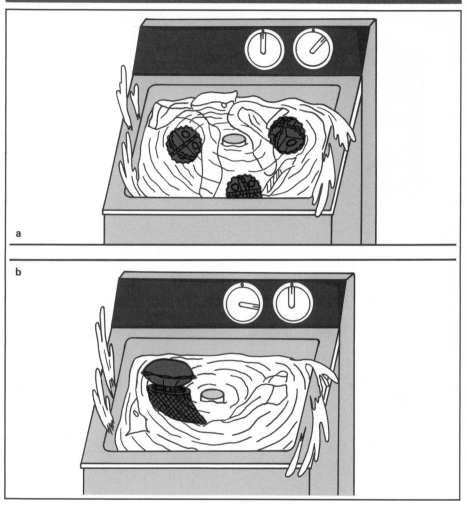

a

b

a   Clothes not getting clean enough?
Add a few Zabu Zabu Balls to your
next wash. These reusable plastic
spheres are designed to create small
areas of turbulence in the wash water, thus intensifying the swirling
cleaning action. Saves on detergent
and also prevents tangles. Sold in flu-
orescent color packs of four at most
supermarkets for ¥380. Do they
work? Japanese housewives swear
by them. . . .

b   Also try Cleaning Balls, inflatable lint
filters that float in your washer ex-
tracting lint and hair from the water
before it can reattach itself to your
clothing. Easy to clean and remove,
these filters cost only ¥215.

CREATIVE HOUSEWARES

a Here is the world's greatest ironing board. It comes with an insulated area to hold the iron and is wide enough to iron an open handkerchief in one motion. The cover and under-cover are washable. The body is made of a mesh material that lets steam circulate better. A specially curved front makes ironing shoul-ders, sleeves, and underarms easier. The legs adjust independently to al-low for uneven floors. A wire shelf below holds supplies or laundry.

b The wonderful world of clothes hang-ers. This one hangs on a pole or clamps onto a line (when hanging outdoors, the clamp prevents the wind from blowing clothes away).

c   With this hanger, when one side is squeezed the other collapses for easy entry into a narrow space like a T-shirt sleeve. It also has a skirt hanger hook attached.

d   These multiple hangers save space; each hanger can also be individually removed. There are also triple-decker hangers, hangers with accessory hooks, and hangers designed for kids' clothing and three-piece suits.

e   Rubber kitchen gloves are sold by left hand, right hand, or in pairs. Other standard items in Japanese stores are aprons with long sleeves, sleeve covers, and upside-down holders for plastic ketchup and mayo containers to help squeeze out every last drop.

COMBINATION TOILET-SINK

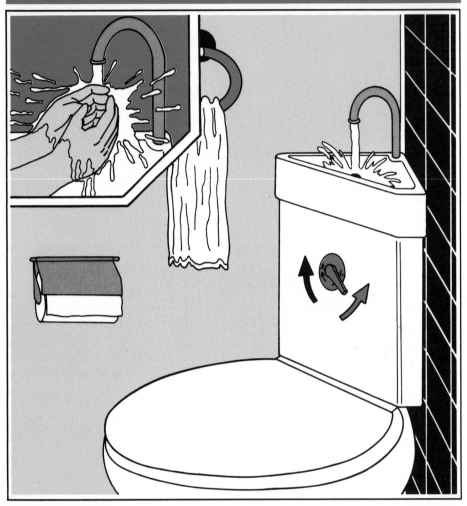

- Turn the handle to the left for a full-tank flush and to the right for a half-tank flush. Then rinse your hands with the water that comes out to re-plenish the tank. Saves space, simplifies plumbing . . . and elimi-nates waste. Invented in 1956, this system costs less than conventional toilets (¥50,000–110,000) and comes in eight- and sixteen-liter sizes and a rainbow of colors. Also available for bathrooms are artificial flushing-sound generators that people can use to cover up the sound of what they're doing without wasting water. One such model is compactly designed to be carried by women in their purses for use outside the home.

TOILET FOR HEMORRHOID SUFFERERS

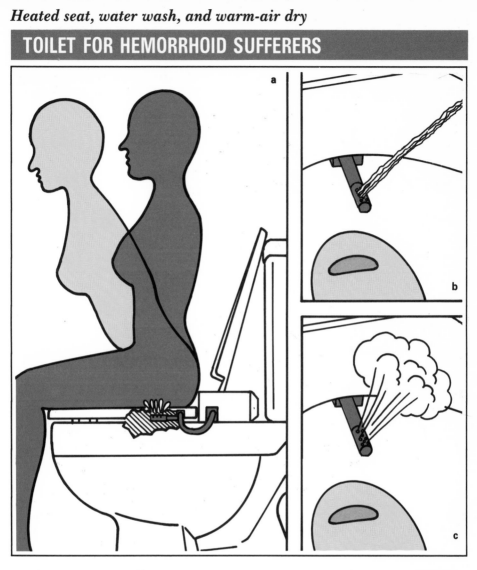

a Good for the long-suffering, the disabled, the sanitation-conscious, and the lazy, the Washlet toilet seat attaches to regular toilet bowls. The seat is thermostatically controlled (good in Japanese homes, many of which lack central heating in winter) and plugs into any standard electrical outlet.

b/c At the push of a button, a nozzle appears and shoots a soft stream of water at your backside, then dries you with warm air. Water and air temperatures are instantly controlled by a built-in ceramic heater. The bidet-style system cleans better than toilet paper. It costs ¥98,000 and comes in ten designer colors.

Water walkers, warmer lids, and a recycling pump

ACCESSORIES FOR THE JAPANESE BATH

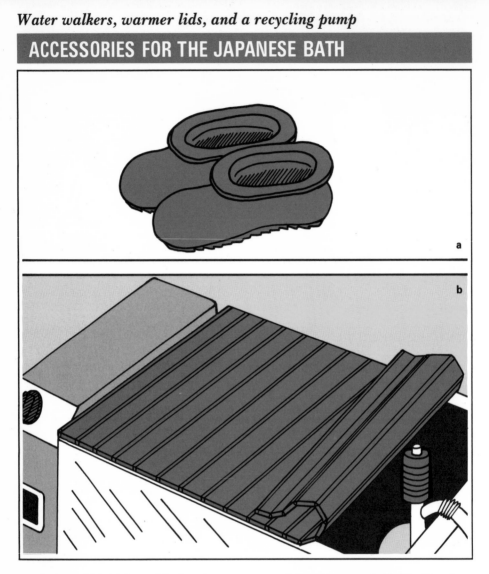

a

b

a   In Japan you wash outside the tub and only get into the tub for soaking. A floor drain takes the soapy wash water away, but the floor stays wet, making it impossible for anyone to go into the bathroom later (to clean or use the sink) without getting their feet wet. The solution: waterproof shoes with plastic uppers and rubber lowers to prevent slipping. One size fits all. Easy on, easy off.

b   Since you don't wash in it, hot bath water can be reused. A lightweight plastic tub cover with foil on one side helps retain heat between soaks. For the ecologically minded: A small electric pump recycles used water to a washing machine or garden hose.

Your personal home spa with real spa water

HOT SPRINGS WATER DELIVERY SERVICE

- Water from Japanese mineral hot springs (called *onsen*) is good for what ails you, but the spas are usually hours outside of town. Solution: A tank truck with water still hot from the ground will deliver it directly from the *onsen* to your home. (The trucks are heavily insulated or use heating elements to keep the water hot en route.) The Kowakien Inn in Hakone (two hours southwest of Tokyo) delivers its own spring water by courier in specially designed twenty-liter boxes. The water comes out of the ground at 197° F and arrives at 113° F, just right for bathing. Contains no sulfur, so it won't harm your bath equipment. A great gift.

INSTANT REJUVENATION AIDS

a   A battery-powered headband cools
    to 15° F below body temperature to
    improve your mental acuity. De-
    signed primarily for grinds at schools
    and universities, the product sells
    more to office workers, doctors, and
    computer hackers. Also recom-
    mended for kitchen slaves and dog
    walkers on a hot summer's day.

b   Liquid body rejuvenators like Estoron
    King and Youthgen King form 50 per-
    cent of some pharmacies' business
    and are also sold at subway kiosks
    and delivered to offices. Prices range
    from ¥150 for a caffeinated vitamin C
    drink to ¥3,000 for a deluxe version
    with ginseng root, royal jelly, viper
    tincture, or rodent and snake organs.

BELLY BANDS, FACE MASKS, AND STRESS GUM

a   Japanese people believe the "soul" resides in the belly, and stomach warmers, made of insulating, stretchy materials that wrap around the waist, are a standard means of keeping well during flu season.

b   Face masks of cotton gauze are worn in winter not to keep germs out of your mouth but as a courtesy to others when you have a cold. They also filter and help warm the air. Fashionable masks now come in pastel colors with messages like "Atchoo!" and "On the road to recovery!"

c   Stress-age Gum uses the body's pH to indicate health. Chew for three minutes. If the gum is dark pink, you're healthy. If it's green, lie down.

A FEW MORE ZANY IDEAS

a   Radicame is a camera on wheels designed to explore things from ground level and to poke its eye where human heads don't belong—according to some users, it is good for looking beneath the skirts of female passersby. Comes with all-automatic focus, flash, and film advance. The lens swivels through 90 degrees. Costs ¥16,000.

b   A Buddhist altar for the home comes with a body temperature sensor. When you sit before the altar it begins chanting sutras through two speakers. If you leave before finishing it will continue the sutra to the end and rewind automatically.

c   Old Japanese picnic boxes were a

marvel of intricacy and compactness, and today's stationery and sewing kits boast the same packaging ingenuity. Team Demi's desk set has scissors, stapler, tape measure, tape dispenser, mat knife, ruler, and glue dispenser, all in a small foam-lined plastic case. Available in eight colors and a big hit in overseas markets.

d Japanese import ice from Antarctica for alcoholic drinks. A Japanese researcher has produced a similar ice in the factory. Filled with slightly compressed air, it "pops" when placed in a beverage, once a second at 70 decibels in 80-proof alcohol, once every two seconds at 65 decibels in whiskey and water.

rvices services services services services services
rvices services services services services services
rvices services services services services services
rvices services services services services services
rvices services services services services services
rvices services services services services services
rvices services services services services services
rvices services services services services services
rvices services services services services services
rvices services services services services services
rvices services services services services services
rvices services services services services services
rvices services services services services services
rvices services services services services services
rvices services services services services services
rvices services services services services services
rvices services services services services services
rvices services services services services services
rvices services services services services services
rvices services services services services services
rvices services services services services services
rvices services services services services services
rvices services services services services services
rvices services services services services services
rvices services services services services services
rvices services services services services services
rvices services services services services services

FULL-SERVICE TAXIS

a   New Yorkers will never believe this. Your hands are full of bags and packages, the cab stops, and the passenger door swings open without your touching it! You climb in and the door swings shut, worked with a simple lever from the driver's seat. When you get out, the door opens for you again. No tipping!

b   Taxi drivers wear white gloves to indicate courtesy, professionalism, and a concern for cleanliness. Speaking of cleanliness, Tokyo taxis are powered by clean propane gas.

c   In some taxis you can sing along to prerecorded music. Drivers like this because it gives inebriated customers something better to do than tell their

life stories.

d   Or you can watch pay TV. Late at night there are samurai movies and variety shows. Great in traffic jams or when you're alone.

e   Most taxis have headrests and seat covers of white lace (provided to the cabs for ¥2,000 a month linen service). Some seats have vibrators to help business people wind down at the end of a stressful day. In the Nagoya area about one hundred fifty taxis are equipped with voice recordings that, when the passenger climbs in, say, "Thank you for taking this cab," and, when he is about to leave, "Please check to make sure you haven't forgotten anything."

HOUSEHOLD MOVING SERVICES

a   Moving doesn't have to be a night-
    mare. If you are a family of six or less,
    you can move to your new home in
    luxury in the same van as your
    household goods. A mobile living
    room sits directly above the driver's
    compartment and comes fully
    equipped with a refrigerator, TV and
    VCR, personal computer, magazines,
    reclining seats, and a view out the
    front. There you sit and dream about
    the new life that awaits you (hence
    the name of the truck, "Dream Sa-
    lon"). While en route you speak with
    the assistant driver by telephone,
    who will answer questions and even
    mix drinks.

b   All your household goods and fur-

nishings are shipped in sealed containers to ensure security and privacy. Once underway, the contents are fumigated for pests, insects, and bacteria.

c Some trucks come equipped with a hydraulic lift for unloading containers directly into second- and third-story apartments. Other services offered by moving companies include interior design and renovation in your new home, disposal of unwanted furniture, working with the electric and gas companies to cancel old and hook up new utilities, subscription forwarding, and "secret moving," so that you can vacate your home before anyone gets wise.

DRIVE-HOME SERVICE

a   Police in Japan are tougher on drunk drivers than police in the United States. To avoid inconvenience, loss of license, and road mishaps, late-night carousers can now pay an escort service to have themselves and their cars taken home. When called by a bartender or a friend, two escorts with a car are dispatched to the scene of the drunk.

b   One escort takes the client home. The other follows in the client's car.

c   The client is seen to his door in safety. When he wakes the next morning he will not have to return to fetch his car, as he might have had he taken a taxi. The escort service costs only 20 percent more than a similar taxi ride.

AIRPORT AND DEPARTMENT STORE COURTESY STAFF

a At some airports, attendants in blue suits and white gloves stand by the machine that collects your boarding pass. They start your trip off right with a bow and a smile (and because they're not preoccupied with collecting the pass, a last security check).

b Japanese companies believe in service from the bottom up. Department stores hire an army of uniformed women whose only job is to attend to customers' needs. Some run elevators and announce the floors. Others stand by the escalator with a handkerchief, constantly wiping the moving rail to keep it clean. Others greet you at the door. Training in speech and manners is intensive.

ELIMINATING BANK LINES

a   Here's an idea American banks should rob. When you enter a Japanese bank, you hand your money and forms to a receptionist, who passes them to a row of clerks for processing. Instead of standing in line while you wait, you can then sit in a comfortable chair, watch TV, sip complimentary tea, or read a magazine. The clerk calls your name when your transaction is complete. No more jangled nerves!

b   Japanese ATMs save time too. You can deposit bills *and* coins, withdraw cash, and even transfer funds from your account to any account in Japan. Insert your passbook, and the ATM will record the new balance.

LAND TRUSTS

- By entering into an agreement with a bank, owners of unused land in Japan can realize a steady income and capital growth without having to sell, develop, or manage the property themselves. The bank tells you what the property is good for: office, residence, convenience store, etc. You then "loan" the land to the bank to develop on your behalf. The bank figures out all the economics, hires the contractor, finds tenants, and manages the property. You get a dividend twice a year. At the end of the "land trust," the property reverts to you. During the term of the trust, you can borrow against the value of the property. A good tax shelter, too.

HANDYMAN AGENCIES

a   There are five hundred *benriya-san* or handyman agencies in Tokyo alone. They charge ¥1,500–3,000 an hour to do anything you need, from household repairs to walking the dog. A handyman will:

b   Shop for you or take care of you when you're sick.

c   Take your jewelry and other valuables to experts for appraisal.

d   Do detective work or shoot videos of you and your partner in bed.

e   Deliver speeches for you or stand in for you at funerals and weddings.

f   Fill out contest and patent applications.

g   Play soccer with your kids or fill in for a sick teammate at a softball game.

HAIRSTYLE PRE-IMAGING AND SCALP MASSAGES

a Many Japanese hair salons use the Hair Simulator to show how any of three hundred hairstyles will look on you. Pick a style from a catalog, punch in its number, look into the monitor, and, *voilà*, there you are on the color screen in your new coif (you can get a print in black and white). Saves time, reduces complaints, improves communication, and is fun to use—try out weird hairstyles! When not simulating haircuts, the machine doubles as a community bulletin board and restaurant guide.

b Many Japanese hair salons start out with a five to fifteen minute scalp massage before cutting begins. Feels wonderful with a shampoo.

FOOD SERVICE AMENITIES

a   Entice customers into your restaurant with realistic PVC models of the food you serve. Custom food models cost about ¥5,000 per dish and are made from photographs or directly from food samples. They are displayed in a glass case (with prices) outside the entrance for passersby to see. Works well for restaurants on second floors, basements, and lightly trafficked streets.

b   Once inside, give your customers a moist, rolled cloth (hot in winter, cool in summer) called an *o-shibori* to wipe face and hands before eating. It is then used as a napkin during the meal. A moment with an *o-shibori* is refreshingly good on a busy day.

HOME FOOD DELIVERY IN REAL DISHES

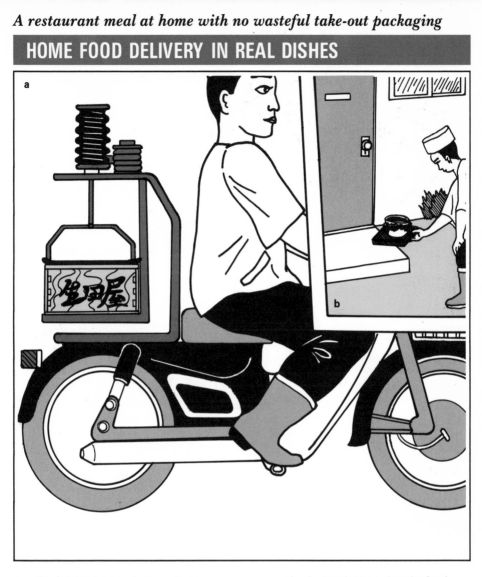

a   For food at home when you're too tired or low on provisions to make it yourself, or wish to entertain a guest with a special, exotic treat, call just about any small restaurant and have a meal delivered to your door in less than half an hour. Delivery men use small motorcycles with a special carrying tray fitted with springs and shock absorbers so that the food doesn't spill en route.

b   Incredibly, the food comes in real glass dishes. You pay the driver, and after eating you leave the dishes—it's polite to rinse them first—outside your door. Several hours later (or the next morning) the driver comes back to collect them.

Hand-crafted ambience for conversation and hanging out

COFFEE SHOP CONCEPTS

a   Lacking private space at home and the office, Japanese go to coffee shops to meet friends and talk business. There are thirty thousand *kissaten* in Tokyo alone. Coffee is expensive (¥150–600 a cup), but you can sit as long as you want. Foods available include cheesecake, sweet gelatin and red beans, chocolate parfaits, mini-pizzas, and cucumber sandwiches. Shops are sometimes devoted to particular themes, like the business *kissaten* Kabutocho in Yokohama, with its industry newspapers and magazines and videotext displays. Buy a cup and you're welcome to use the Quotron.

b   One type of shop caters to young

lovers. Booths are designed for forced intimacy and privacy, with discreet service, soft lighting, and seats on only one side of the table.

c   A Tokyo coffee shop offers office workers a place to take a nap after a hard day on the front lines.

d   Many shops are devoted exclusively to certain types of music: classical,

1950s jazz, blues. At some, talking is not permitted. Owners install high-end sound equipment and obtain the latest releases. Current audio journals (as well as a large supply of comic books) are available for reading. Most music *kissaten* also have request forms that patrons can use to select their favorite tunes.

TINY BARS

- After food and before catching the last train home, many Japanese businessmen stop off at their favorite bars, called "snacks." Some parts of town, like Shinjuku and Shinbashi in Tokyo, have hundreds of bars all crowded in together, each measuring only fifty to one hundred square feet and containing nothing more than a counter, some chairs, a rack of liquor, and a hot plate for making appetizers. Strangers rarely wander in off the street but are introduced by like-minded patrons, who mostly come for conversation with the host, usually a woman. Her personality and musical taste create most of the bar's homey, comforting atmosphere.

BOTTLE KEEP AND ENDLESS APPETIZERS

a   **How to guarantee return customers,
    Japanese style:** Many bars in Japan
    keep customers' personal bottles of
    whiskey for them between visits.
    Bars sell the bottles for ¥4,000–9,000
    or more, and make additional money
    by charging for ice and water. Some
    Japanese have bottles in dozens of
    bars. Having a bottle in an exclusive
    club can be a mark of status.

b   *Shochu* is a distilled alcohol made
    from just about anything vegetable.
    One Tokyo *shochu* bar has over 650
    varieties, and offers tempting appe-
    tizers on "boats" that float by as you
    drink: great impulse eating and in-
    stant gratification at two bucks a
    plate.

Clean, safe places for people who just need a place to sleep

CAPSULE HOTELS

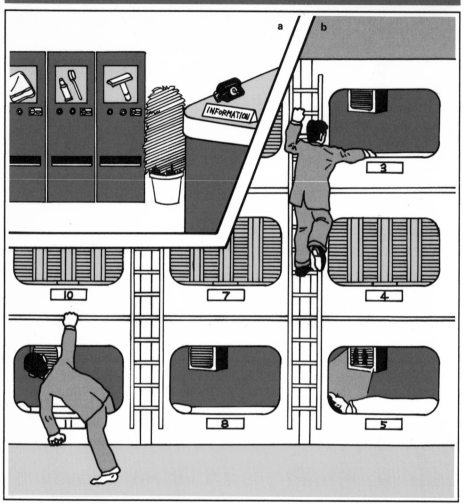

a Working late at the office? Trains on strike? Miss the last bus home? Can't face the long commute only to have to wake up early the next morning and do the same thing all over again? Stay in a capsule hotel: basic amenities in a prefab, Pullman-style sleeping compartment, at a price 20 to 50 percent less than a normal business hotel. For maximum convenience, the front desk is staffed twenty-four hours a day, and razors, soap, snacks, and a host of other supplies are available in vending machines in the lobby. Check in after 5 P.M., check out before 9 A.M. These stripped-down sleepers generally are located near train and subway stations and

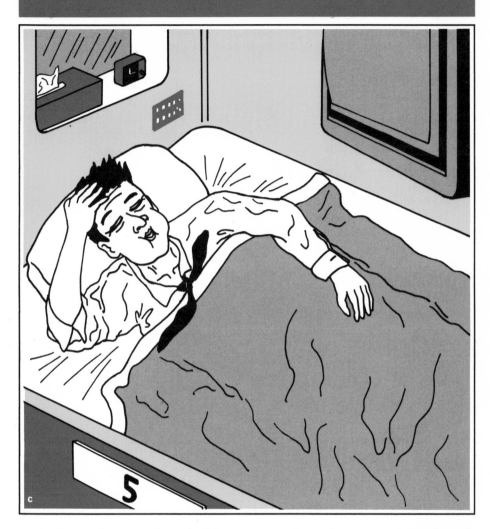

have proved enormously successful in Japan, where bars are open late and public transportation stops running early. Managers like them because they are easy to clean and maintain and cost only about ¥700,000 per capsule to buy and install. Similar capsule set-ups might conceivably be used as housing for the needy or for people forced out of their homes by fire or flood.

b   Sleeping capsules are stacked two to three high.

c   Each capsule comes with a TV, radio, alarm clock, reading light, small shelf, and entrance closure for privacy. A shower room is on the main floor. Only one person allowed per capsule.

COIN SNEAKER LAUNDRY

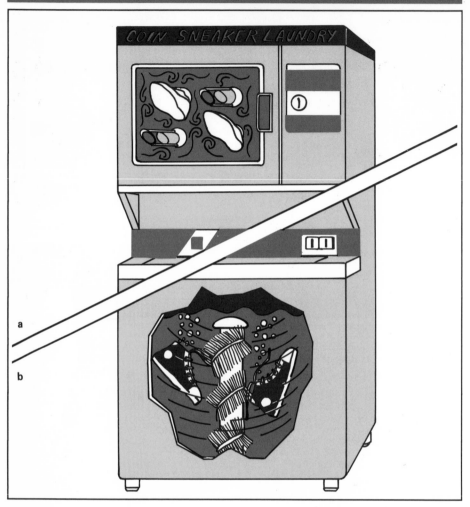

a   Freshly washed sneakers feel great, but putting them in the clothes washer can damage the machine. So the Japanese have invented a machine just for washing sneakers and running shoes. The dryer unit (pictured here) stacks atop the washer. One drying cycle takes twenty minutes for footwear made out of synthetic material and forty minutes for tennis or high-top canvas shoes. Low heat prevents damage to the soles. An ultraviolet light disinfects.

b   The washing unit uses vinyl brushes and a special detergent that kills germs. It does two pairs of adult shoes or four pairs of children's shoes at a time.

SAFETY-BOX UNDERWEAR LAUNDRY

- The pitch here is that intimate apparel demands an especially discreet cleaning. At the Men's Clean Koenji shop, ¥1,000 buys a key to one of 240 small mailbox-like compartments. In your compartment you place dirty underwear, along with a ticket showing you have paid ¥100 for each pair. Mysteriously, by noon of the second day after your visit, your underwear is back in your compartment, folded and clean. One problem apartment-dwelling women in Japan face are "panty thieves," fetishists who snatch their underwear off clotheslines at night. It was perhaps to combat such mischief that this business was created.

Relax, get clean, socialize, and soak yourself silly

COMMUNITY PUBLIC BATHS

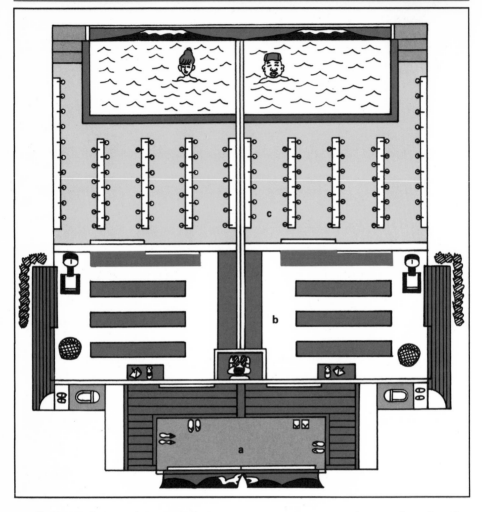

a   You're rarely more than a ten-minute walk away from a public bath in Japan. Here neighbors gather for a communal soak at the end of the day, steaming away their cares and catching up on local gossip. The original hot tub! (Literally; the water is kept at about 104° F.) A visit costs ¥270; stay as long as you like. Enter at (*a*),

remove your shoes, and put them in a locker.

b   Now go into the changing room, left side for women, right side for men. Pay the attendant, who sits in the middle of the two sides by the door. On sale are sundries like soap, towels, razors, and cool drinks. Outside may be a terrace and a small garden

for cooling off after the bath.

c   This is the washing area, with rows of hot and cold water taps, shower heads, stools, and plastic buckets.

d   First, sit at one of the taps and rinse yourself off with water. Then go to the main tub, soak for a few minutes to get warm, and return to the taps for soaping and serious washing, using the shower and a hand towel. Now go back and soak again. Repeat as necessary. Some baths have a regular tub for soaking and another Jacuzzi-like tub for water massage. The back wall is often decorated with a large, panoramic mural, paid for by local merchants (whose advertising is painted along its base). Truly poetic.

PAPER-RECYCLING TRUCK

- A familiar sound in Japanese neighborhoods is the taped announcement and jingle of the *chirigami kokan* truck, which alerts everyone to bring out their old newspapers, magazines, cardboard boxes, and fabrics for disposal. In exchange the driver gives out rolls of toilet paper (or tissue) according to the weight of the material he collects. Profitability of this venture is tied to the current price of paper, so the number of recyclers is always changing. Japanese have indicated they would support recycling even without the free toilet paper, because it eliminates burning costs (paid by taxes) and helps reduce air pollution.

TELEPHONE SERVICES FOR BUSY PEOPLE

a   More and more Japanese conduct their business on the phone while on the run. Service industries are emerging to exploit this fast-paced way of life. Alibi Makers, for example, provides you with ready-made excuses. They will call your spouse as if calling from your company (with believable office sound effects) to say you won't be home this evening. They also provide wake-up calls.

b   The company Today keeps your personal diary. You call up and tell a tape recorder what you did that day (meetings, contracts, lunch, and so on). Each month, Today transcribes the tape and sends you a record of your activities in an attractive binder.

COSMETIC SURGERY TO IMPROVE YOUR LIFE

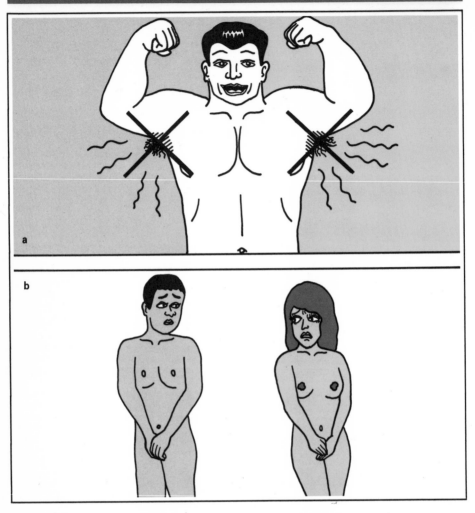

a   In Japan, women with body odor are said to have a hard time getting married. The solution? Go to the Jujin Clinic in Tokyo and for ¥250,000 have your offending sweat glands removed. Located in the high-rent Ginza district, the clinic looks more like a beauty salon: pink decor, with nurses in pale pink uniforms.

b   The Jujin Clinic also offers surgery on sex organs. Circumcision costs ¥150,000. Sewing up the hymen to "restore" virginity costs ¥120,000. Making the vagina smaller to reduce the stretch from childbirth costs ¥400,000. Jujin doesn't recommend implanting a pearl into the tip of the penis, but will do the job if asked.

Change your car "ordinaire" into an import "exceptionnel"

AUTOMOBILE BODY CLONING

a   Spend ¥395,000 and buy a Corvetti Kit that will turn your lowly Mazda RX7 into a sparkling Corvette. Installation is about ¥250,000, takes several people an entire day, and includes a paint job.

b   The Mad House garage in Shizuoka Prefecture sells a kit called Aeroparts that turns a Toyota MR2 body into a BMW (from certain angles at least). It improves airflow, they say. Other Mad House kits turn a Honda City body into a French Renault 5 Turbo and a Mazda RX7 into a Porsche 935. "We're not counterfeiters, we're parodists," the car cloners claim. "We hope the comic effect of remodeling will be understood."

BAR CONCEPTS

a   The bar Pardennen in Kobe has an approach to pricing that has proved very popular: It charges for the time spent on its premises, not for the amount of liquor consumed. You pay ¥500 for the first ten minutes, and ¥30 (men) or ¥20 (women) for each additional minute. Dance discos in Japan often charge at the door and provide unlimited food and drink buffets inside. Waiters like this because they don't have to worry about remembering tabs.

b   The bar Maruchi Yokaden in Osaka wants to attract families, and has installed a nursery with video games, picture books, and two female attendants.

Eat, drink, and maybe win a prize!

RESTAURANT PROMOTIONS

a Tokyo is full of restaurants, and many have taken to offering special promotions in the hope of attracting customers. One restaurant catering to students in Kanda, Tokyo, offers a ¥50 refund if you eat all your food. They have a sign on the wall: "If you want smaller portions, speak up!"

b At the Ribera restaurant in Tokyo, eat three one-pound steaks and three plates of rice in half an hour and get the meal for free, plus ¥10,000. At Dairy Chiko, finish a ten-inch-tall ice cream cone in an hour and you won't have to pay.

c Otoya in Osaka offers free food items according to the day of the week, the time of day, and the season.

SADISTIC CUISINES

a   On the southeast coast of Honshu is found the Cruel Grill cuisine. Clam-shaped pearl oysters called *apapa* are placed on the grill while still alive, and as they fry their shells pop open and shut, making the sound of their name. Shrimp and other shellfish are also broiled alive here. In the Moan Grill cuisine, live abalone writhe around the surface of the grill as they sear, the visual display bringing delight to fish aficionados.

b   In Hell Tofu cuisine, a bowl of boiling broth is loaded with cold tofu and eel-shaped fish called *dojo*. The fish seek refuge from the heat in the tofu, but to no avail, and the resultant *dojo* tofu is said to be quite tasty.

CATCH-AS-CATCH-CAN CUISINE

- *Somen* are very thin wheat noodles, like angel hair pasta. Originated by aristocrats in the old capital of Kyoto, they are among connoisseurs considered the most stylish and tasteful, a quality the Japanese call *iki*. And what could be more stylish than *nagashi somen* ("flowing noodles") in summer? The noodles are placed in a flume carrying clear, ice cold water. As the *somen* pass by, you pluck them out with your chopsticks, deftly dip them in a container of sauce, and guide them to your mouth. The most excruciatingly chic places put their *somen* in real streams: a variation on the well-known sushi-boat restaurants.

ONE INGREDIENT, MULTICOURSE RESTAURANTS

- Some restaurants focus not on a single cuisine but on a single ingredient, and go to great lengths to create a meal with it that is tasty and varied in flavor, texture, and appearance. Here are some dishes served at a restaurant specializing in bamboo.

a   Bamboo shoot and seasoned rice.

b   Bamboo shoot boiled and sliced and eaten with a dipping sauce.

c   Cold bamboo shoot mixed with other vegetables and chicken.

d   Bamboo clear broth soup.

e   Bamboo shoot tempura.

f   Bamboo shoot salad (or bamboo shoot omelet roll, or bamboo shoot and seaweed, and so on and so on and so on).

The ultimate in have-it-your-way cuisine

COOK-IT-YOURSELF RESTAURANTS

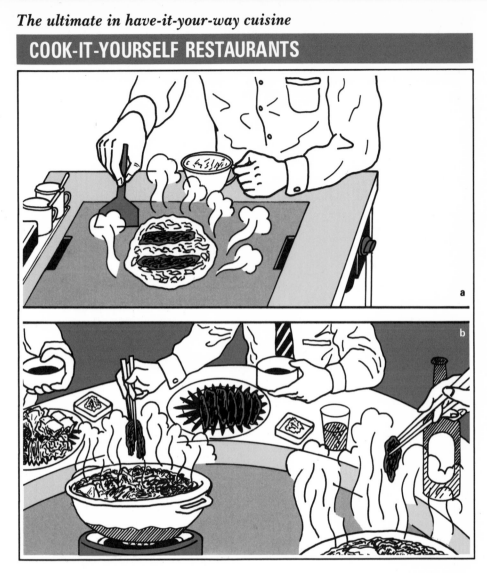

a   Here's an idea for restaurant owners who can't keep good chefs: Make the customers cook their own food. That's what happens with *okono-miyaki*, Japanese pancakes with various "fillings." You sit at a low table with a griddle. Waiters bring the fixings: flour, egg, and cabbage with your choice of shrimp, vege-tables, ham, etc. You mix the batter, pour it on the hot griddle, top the pancake with sauce, and eat. Cheap.

b   Another good winter dish is *nabemono*. You and your party sit around a bowl of hot broth and add fresh ingredients (noodles, fish, greens) to make a rich and flavorful communal stew. Season to taste.

77

At last, enjoy restaurant food made the way you like it

RENTAL RESTAURANTS

a A new concept in restaurateuring. The Grand Chef Rental Restaurant in Ginza asks patrons to come in and cook their own food for large parties. It is especially popular among top company executives who belong to cooking clubs and use the kitchen as a chance to practice their skills by making food for their employees at the office. The restaurant provides all the dishware, but customers provide the food.

b Grand Chef Rental Restaurant holds a maximum of thirty-eight people and is only seven hundred square feet in area (less than half of it kitchen). A meal for ten costs ¥33,000 base price plus ¥2,000 per person.

Fun at the top, with a view and entertainment al fresco

ROOFTOP BEER GARDENS

- In summer, many office buildings and department stores turn their vast open roofs into beer gardens, an example of how this very special urban space can be put to exceptionally good use. Sitting here you feel above the bustle, a bit romantic, and if you're lucky the height will catch a soothing summer breeze. The cuisine here is mostly finger food, often German in origin (reflecting the strong beer hall influence). Music is provided by recordings or by very mediocre live bands. At either side of the stage one often finds young women dancing in brief costumes. Usually only one brand of beer is on draft, and it is consumed in extraordinary quantity.

RESTAURANTS ON WHEELS

a   Food wagons called *yatai* attract late-night revelers on their way home. Along with hot sake and beer, *yatai* offer a variety of traditional favorites like *oden* stew, noodles, and skewered chicken. Panels fold out to form a narrow counter, and customers sit on a bench or stools as they eat. Hard to resist and very cheap.

b   Serving the trendy section of Daikanyama in Tokyo is a French restaurant in a converted four-ton freezer truck. Seating up to ten, it opens at 9 P.M. and departs between three and five in the morning. A dozen dishes are on the menu, with bread, wine, and cheese. The truck becomes open air in summer.

THEME TRAIN CARS

a   Amtrak pay attention! Japan Railways offers travel packages including food and hotel, and along the way it will carry you and your group in special "Joyful Cars," which don't resemble railway cars at all.

b   For example, ride in a car outfitted like a Japanese room, where you sit on tatami and drink and eat. One car has a Japanese garden. Some have floor shows. Open-air cars give the feeling of riding on an outdoor patio. The Salon Express resembles the lobby of a fancy hotel. The Orient Saloon recreates an antique European train. Theme cars are a great promotion, and the railroad charges a premium for their use.

Why waste space when there's money to be made?

STORES BENEATH TRAINS AND ROADBEDS

- Japanese retailers are quick to seize every space imaginable. A little corner six by six feet with a counter and a few stools can with a little work be made into a bar, a shoe repair shop, a video parlor, a florist's, a fortune teller's, or a warehouse. As a result of this low-tech approach, much of the prime real estate beneath the elevated trains and highways that run through Japanese cities has been commandeered by merchant squatters. Generally dark and noisy, these spaces nevertheless offer vital services (like pachinko pinball games) to the tens of thousands of commuters who pass by daily on their way to and from the nearby train stations.

At night many eating places set grill tables and benches right out on the sidewalk in the hope of enticing customers to pause for a quick beer and piece of fish or fried tofu. Here the rich and poor mingle together, their conversations lost in the hammering sounds of the traffic overhead. While there is nothing revolutionary about using such spaces, the Japanese approach is refreshingly free of most municipal entanglements, since exactly who owns the land is not clear. Legally it belongs to Japan Railways, but tenants have de facto usage rights by virtue of occupying it. The result is pioneer grubstake entrepreneuring.

VENDING MACHINES

A low rate of streetside vandalism and a national obsession with maximum convenience have made Japan the vending machine capital of the world. Machines are everywhere and dispense—in addition to candy and soda—computer software, panty hose, whiskey, hot sake, audio CDs, batteries, magazines, rice, and video cassettes, to name but a few items. One machine sells pearls (for ¥5,000–30,000) so that "young men needn't be embarrassed in jewelry shops about buying the less expensive variety." Some machines have voice boxes that thank you for the purchase and ask you to come again. Other machines tempt passersby

with roulette-style games. Insert money, select the item you want, and an electronic wheel starts spinning; if it stops on the lucky number you win a free selection. Rows of vending machines at train stations provide important goods and services late at night when everything else is closed. One of the more interesting varieties is the magazine vending machine. Often harmless newsweeklies are sold in these. But some sell porno, and these machines are usually fitted with a mirrorlike finish that prevents the contents from being seen by passing children. Outside many neighborhood pharmacies are condom vending machines.

"Fusion" approach sells unlikely juxtapositions of goods

CROSS MERCHANDISING

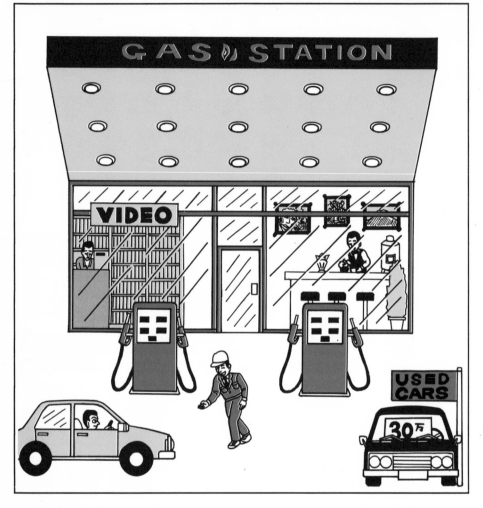

- The "fusion" business shown here is a combination of gas station, video sales and rental shop, café, art gallery, and used car lot. In fusion businesses, Japanese retailers are looking for a synergistic effect, where one merchandise or service spins off to add allure and market to the others. Other examples: bookstore + variety store + haberdashery + used cars and motorcycles (Nagoya); pool hall + bookstore + bowling alley + video shop + film developer + noodle restaurant (Osaka); car dealer + family restaurant + ice cream parlor + convenience store (Hiratsuka); athletic club + aesthetic salon + beauty shop + dentist (Tokyo).

FOOD AND CROP FUTURES

- As a source of working capital, Japanese farmers sell shares in their output to city dwellers who want really fresh produce but who have no time to fetch it themselves. For example, a Tokyo supermarket sells rights to the entire annual output of a single apple tree for ¥25,000. The shareholder is welcome to go pick the apples himself, but if he can't the farmer will package and send them at no extra charge. Similarly, for ¥8,000 per turkey, a farmer will feed, slaughter, and send it to you in December. Invest in timber stands, and as an additional premium you will receive regional food shipments and discounts at local inns.

INDEPENDENT KINGDOMS

a Hoshinokuni ("Star Country"). The
developer of this 950-unit condo
made it into an independent country
to foster a sense of community. It
now has a president, a foreign minis-
ter (to deal with surrounding lands),
an information ministry, and treaties
with local retailers for discounts.

b Jipangu-koku, Aizu, Ashinomaki-han
in Fukushima Prefecture functions
like a kingdom of two hundred years
ago, when this was a well-known
city. Now all six hundred residents
dress in samurai garb and play their
part—all day, every day.

c The Republic of Nikko Nikko came
into being to reclaim tourists after
the high-speed bullet train passed

the town by. Over forty-two days ¥20 million was spent to "open" the nation, with games, sports events, and merchandising of souvenirs. The gas station became the Arabian Embassy, the striptease joint became the National Dance Theater, and the plumber became the Chief of Industrial Technology. In one year tourism increased 155 percent; business was up 300 to 500 percent.

d   Survival Country in Akita offers a primitive experience and a lodge with no gas, water, or electricity.

e   Manga Kingdom in Nagano is devoted to comics (*manga*). Its Royal Nap Library is for dozing while reading. Artists are honorary ministers.

SELECTED-ITEM CONSUMER DAYS

a   In the absence of a holiday, invent one. Almost 25 percent of all Japanese chocolate sales each year are for Valentine's Day, February 14. The custom in Japan on this day is for girls to give gifts to boys. The candy industry thus invented White Day for March 14, to prolong the buying spree and switch it over to boys, who are expected to buy something white for their girlfriends to repay them for their kindness: soap, flowers, underwear, a gift wrapped in white paper, and, of course, white chocolate.

b   Vendors also confected Ice Cream Day, May 9, with three scoops for the price of two. November 10 is Toilet Day (buy a new toilet!).

CONVENIENT FOODSTUFF PACKAGING

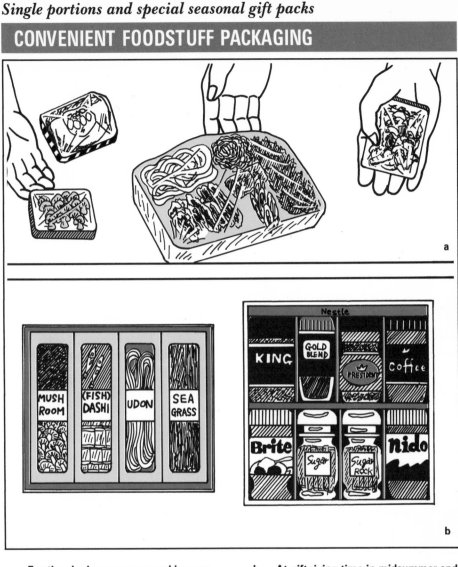

a

b

a For the single person or working couple, no more dead vegetables in the fridge! Many younger Japanese live alone and keep odd hours, and grocers have begun to cater to them by packaging food in small portions: a quarter head of lettuce, or a mix of vegetables that offers a balanced meal with no waste.

b At giftgiving time in midsummer and early December, department stores are filled with convenient and appealing food packs. A combo pack of dried *shiitake* mushrooms, *udon*, and dried kelp for making noodle dishes costs ¥5,000. You can also buy seaweed sets, salad oil sets, rice cracker sets, coffee sets, and dozens more.

NOVELTY LIQUOR, BEER, AND SAKE PACKAGING

a **Here is a self-heating sake can. Pull a grenade pin on the base to start a chemical reaction that warms the drink. Good at ball games.**

b **Some beers celebrate famous people and events. The can of Sapporo here commemorates the opening of the "bullet train" line between Tokyo and Sendai.**

c **The Kirin Beer Shuttle is a gimmick container, as are the giant egg, bamboo stalk, and robot containers.**

d **Cobra Whiskey aims at a young audience and features illustrations of hard-boiled heroes in the style of American comic books.**

e **Sake comes in one-liter coated cardboard containers. Put the carton in**

hot water, and read the temperature of the sake off the thermometer on its side.

f   The Suntory penguin has been the most popular promotion device to date. Besides the penguin-shaped container, standard Suntory packages have shown penguins around the world playing tennis, baseball, or golf. Package designs change with the season.

g   Kirin Beer makes a mini-barrel with the head of a mythical beast for its spout as well as mini-cans for women and micro-cans for lunch. Suntory Beer makes thirty-four containers for every possible occasion and consumer.

PACKAGING OF EVERYDAY PRODUCTS

a

b

c

a   Packaging is a statement, so why not make it your own? The Audio Cassette Cover Kit contains everything you need to customize your favorite tapes for yourself or as a gift. The package includes high-quality photos of exotic vistas (the South Seas, Manhattan) with adhesive backing, a mailing envelope for sending it to a friend, and press-on label lettering.

b   Packaging also relies on creating new product associations. Clothes can be sold in "picture windows." A rigid, dark-colored plastic frame and clear plastic envelope press tightly against a shirt or pair of underwear, making it into a form of visual art.

c   Batteries sold in bulk in clear plastic

cylinders trigger off new product associations: Don't they resemble a kind of food or snack stick? Packs offer all popular sizes of batteries and are easy to stack and store.

d   Clever packaging of women's panties looks like ice cream cones.

e   *Natto* (fermented soy beans) is still sold in a package made of straw.

Leaves, branches, husk, and bark are often used in traditional Japanese packaging, and today have the folksy appeal of being anti-ultraslick.

f   Household repair items are often packaged in logical pairings. The package here contains caulking and a roll of masking tape, since these two items are generally used together.

COORDINATED STATIONERY SYSTEMS

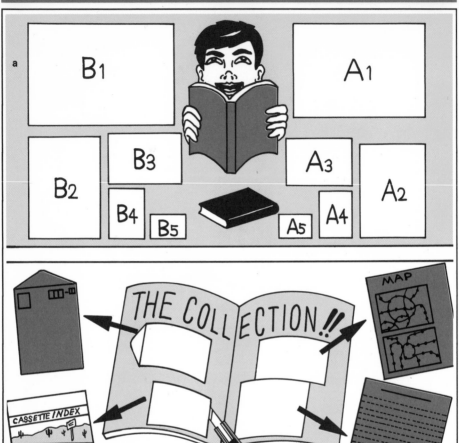

a All paper in Japan is sized according to two standard formats, A and B. A1 and B1 are the largest sheets in each series, with smaller sizes figured in half steps. A2, for example, is half the size of A1, A3 is half the size of A2, and so on. A4 size is 210 mm x 297 mm, about the size of typing paper. Standard sizes make it cheaper to plan printing and warehousing.

b *The Collection* is a stationery "store" sold as a magazine. Bound into it are postcards, envelopes, grid pad, address book, letter pad, traffic map, guide to live music, cassette index, gift box, bookkeeping notebook, book covers, etc. Periodic new editions have all new merchandise.

● Unlike the cheap generic goods sold in American groceries, the plain, tan-color merchandise sold at the Mujirushi Ryohin chain of stores has style and quality. Most items cost 20 to 30 percent less than the brand-name variety, but are by no means bottom of the line. Recycled materials are used whenever possible. The FOOD section offers pasta, dried vegetables, nuts, dried fish, coffee, spices. WEAR sells workshirts, jeans, sneakers, and accessories, but only a few kinds each season. HOME has storage systems, window shades, toothbrushes, cushions, stationery, bicycles. Simplicity, necessity, and conscionable consumerism.

PREPAID DESIGNER TELEPHONE CARDS

- To phone companies, prepaid phone cards represent money received in advance for services not yet rendered. The more cards sold, and the fewer cards used, the higher the profit to the phone company. That's the idea, and the result is a whole new entrepreneurial industry in Japan.

a Prepaid cards come in denominations of ¥500, ¥1,000, and ¥3,000. Insert the card into a public phone to make a call. When you hang up, the card returns with holes punched to show how much time remains.

b The basic card with fifty units showing. Each unit equals one local call.

c NTT (the phone company) issues twenty new designs each month.

Independent publishers using NTT blanks issue another thousand. Scenic landscapes are popular designs.

d   So are cartoon characters.

e   And historical and folkart themes.

f   Cards showing celebrities, especially teenage idols, are highly prized.

g   Cards as advertising medium. A person can buy blanks and print them up to give to clients as business cards: "If you need to call me for any reason, use this." Cards are also given as premiums with purchases in stores.

h   Cards are traded like stamps, and some have become valuable collectors items. Every month a guide is issued to the collecting scene with news about cards old and new.

ALL-ORACLE BUILDING

- Many Japanese turn to fortune tellers for advice on education, finance, love, and naming children. In Tokyo's trendy Harajuku section, a building where thirteen fortune tellers are on call at any one time, each in his or her own parlor, is open from 11 A.M. to 8 P.M. every day of the week, and twenty-four hours on the day before New Year's. The smorgasbord of prophecies includes Chinese systems like the I-Ching and other systems from around the world like Tarot, astrology, geomancy, and palmistry. There are two hundred in all. Buy a ticket at the entrance. Cost for twenty minutes of advice ranges from ¥1,000 to ¥3,000, depending on age.

COUNTRY BUMPKIN TOURS

a   A Tokyo travel agent has developed a tour to introduce rich farmers from the provincial Japanese countryside to the capital's modern ways. "New Style Tour to Find New Culture" costs ¥1 million for three days.

b   First, the farmers receive fashionable haircuts.

c   Then they're dropped off—without escort—in Harajuku, the city's avant-garde fashion district, where they shop for the designer clothes they will need to get into a snotty disco in the Aoyama district.

d   ... but only three of them will be allowed entry. The tour developer says the insult is part of the experience.

e   And then to bed at a deluxe hotel.

LOVE HOTELS

a   Japan's trysting spots for quickies
    and all-night pleasures are often dis-
    tinguished by their purple neon signs
    and flamboyant exteriors, which can
    look like medieval castles, luxury
    ocean liners, or space ships. They
    cost ¥3,500–10,000 per hour and
    ¥4,500–20,000 (and up) for over-
    night. Some hotels have sex manual

and paraphernalia shops, Polaroid
camera rentals, and uniforms so you
can dress up as a nurse, sailor, police
officer, or doctor. There is generally
a vending machine that dispenses
condoms.

b   Every effort is made to ensure your
    privacy and anonymity. Hotel staff
    are virtually invisible. You park and

enter from a garage lot that has a curtain so your license plate can't be seen from the street. You can check in and out entirely by computer. One hotel has an outdoor computer-linked sign that reads, "Sorry, rooms are full now. Estimated waiting time forty-five minutes."

c   The Alpha Inn in Tokyo has twenty-six rooms and specializes in S/M decor. Each room has a name and theme: Marquis de Sade, Doctor's Office, Insane Crucifix, Slave Market.

d   More benign love hotel rooms might have bathrooms with water slides, revolving beds, and mirrored everything. The latest trend, however, is to more refined and elegant decor.

THEME WEDDINGS

a   Weddings in Japan are elaborate affairs that require careful planning. An agency does much of the work, from selecting rings to finding the newlyweds an apartment. It also selects the wedding hall, where the ceremony can be performed with considerable panache, complete with theatrical events and an emcee who keeps everyone entertained with fast patter about married life as he pokes fun at the bride and groom. Shown here, a gondola introduces the spotlit couple as it floats them from ceiling to floor through a sea of dry-ice.

b   At some receptions, there is a ten-minute slide show on the lives of the bride and groom from birth. If the

parents of the happy couple don't cry at this point, some emcees won't accept a fee for the day.

c   Darken the lights, and the wedding hall becomes a planetarium. Here the newlyweds look on as the emcee explains how the auspicious constellations signal a happy marriage.

d   At the reception the bride and groom change their clothes three times (wedding kimono, dress kimono, Western formal wear). The couple shown here pounds rice into a loaf to serve to all the guests as the first act of their life together.

e   At the end of the reception, everyone goes outside the hall to let helium balloons off into the sky.

Low-tech pedal power and mazes are high-fun attractions

THEME PARK CONCEPTS

a

a   The Gunma Sports Cycle Center, located in a national forest, is devoted exclusively to the concept of bicycling and pedal power. A ski lift takes you from the parking lot to the activity area, where there are weird bicycles for one, two, or three people (seesaw bicycles, a round bicycle with a table and umbrella in the middle, lopsided bicycles, unicycles), a train and monorail that move by pedal power alone, and a pedal-powered skyride (thirteen feet above ground) and roller coaster. A three-mile bicycle trail winds through the woods, but you are required to take a twenty-minute class in bicycle safety before you go. Low energy and fun.

b

b   Mazes are another energy-efficient entertainment in Japan. The most famous is the Gran Maze in Kyoto, which twists and turns over the area of a football field with bridges and tall wall dividers. As you race through you get stamps at four checkpoints. Fastest time is twelve minutes. Longest is five hours (there are emergency exits along the way). Some schools and companies take maze field trips, and there are maze clubs and annual maze meets. At Expoland in Osaka the maze has a Western theme, and players go through a covered wagon entryway to find the cowboys, Indians, and outlaws who mark the checkpoints.

HOT SPRINGS ATTRACTIONS

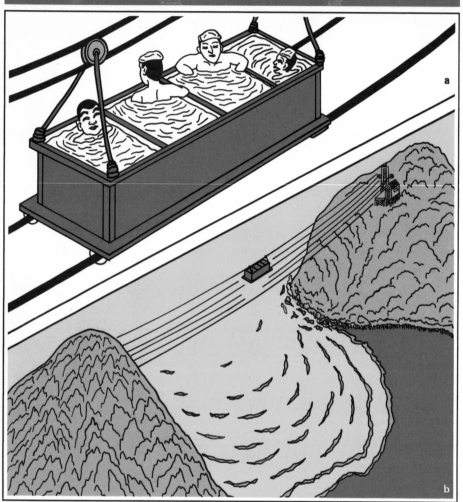

a

b

a/b Japan is geothermically active, and hot springs, called *onsen*, abound. Many springs are considered of medical benefit, but most are places to cavort and relax. Resort developers constantly devise new ways of attracting customers. At the Arita Kanko Hotel in Wakayama, the Amazing Universal Apollo Bath features an aerial cable car with soaking tubs and a superb view of the ocean and bay. Meanwhile, inside Arita, you can go from a bath in warm sake, to a waterfall bath, to a milk bath featuring a giant plastic cow at poolside, to a revolving bath shaped like a tangerine. You end at the flower bath, where you sit amidst richly colored petals.

c   At Takaragawa Onsen in Gunma Pre-
    fecture you bathe along with seven
    tame (you hope) bear cubs that be-
    long to the owner of the inn. A
    similar experience awaits you at
    Jigokudani Onsen in Nagano Prefec-
    ture, where monkey families come
    down from the surrounding nature
    preserve to join you and frolic in the
    outdoor tub.

d   In the winter at Shikaribetsu Kogami
    Onsen in Hokkaido, a wooden tub is
    anchored in a hole cut out of a two-
    foot-thick frozen lake surface. Hot
    bath water is piped in, and you sit en-
    joying the snow and glacial view
    while sipping sake or some of the
    fine regional wine.

JAPANESE INNS

a

b

a *Ryokan* are Japanese-style hotels for travelers. They differ from Western-style hotels in a number of important respects. Hospitality is one. You are greeted at the entryway, shown to your room, and immediately given a warm cup of tea or refreshing soft drink. You are then urged to go for a soak in the communal tub. In the evening, lavish fresh-cooked meals (included in the price) are served in your room. One of the staff is on hand to explain the regional specialties and describe the local sights.

b After dinner the hotel staff remove the dishes. As you once more frolic in the bath, the staff enter your room and remove your futon from the clos-

ets to lay them out on the tatami for sleeping. A whole family stays in one room. Rooms are also set aside for carousing men on holiday. At New Year's the staff dress in formal wear and present the guests with sweets.

c   You can arrive with virtually nothing in the way of baggage. Once in your room you are given a distinctive *yukata* robe, a handtowel, a razor, and a toothbrush with toothpaste already embedded in its bristles. Since the main recreation at a country *ryokan* is the hot springs bath, you spend most of your time in your robe. Shown here are two gentlemen, each in the robe of his inn, each heading for his respective bath.

ULTRA-PERSISTENT VIDEO HARD SELL

a The never-say-die approach to marketing video cameras and VCRs. ABC Camera of Osaka has contracted with the amusement park Expoland (on the site of the 1970 exposition) to operate a small booth next to the main ticket booth. There, for a special price, you buy a ticket to the park and rent a video camcorder.

b In an adjacent tent, ABC Camera staff show you how to shoot video and give you a free blank tape.

c You spend the day at Expoland with your kid; like any proud parent you record his every move.

d Before leaving the park you return the camcorder to the ABC Camera tent. Toys are there for your kid to

play with, and while he does you are shown the video you've just taken, given refreshments, praised for your talents with the camera, and counseled about how to improve. You are asked for your phone number.

e A few weeks later you get a phone call. "Now we're offering a 40 percent discount on video equipment. It's a great time to buy." Two months later, two ABC Camera salesmen (including one you met at Expoland) come to your house. They give a stuffed doll to your child and begin another demo, shooting around the house. Finally they show you the video on your own TV, wearing down the last of your resistance. You buy.

DEPARTMENT STORE MERCHANDISING TIPS

a Japanese department stores are clever. Sometimes they don't put escalators next to each other but at a distance, so that customers going up or down walk through sales areas.

b Stores never miss an opportunity to broadcast a buy message. Video monitors are used extensively, often in banks of a dozen. Ambient videos create a mood on the floor; point of purchase videos are at registers.

c Stores take total control of a consumer's life and are often but a piece in a network of related businesses. Some of the very big networks own the rail and bus lines that bring customers into the city (the flagship store is the terminus). They own

the baseball teams customers root for. They also own land along the railways, developing it for housing to create a captive customer base and profits from land values.

d   Foreign customer liaison departments help non-Japanese customers find what they're looking for, and also offer services not sold in the store, like language lessons, moving, and storage. Membership entitles foreigners to discounts at store-sponsored events.

e   Employees at one store wear badges that say "Veteran Golfer" or "Flower Arranger" to identify their hobbies so that customers can relate to them on a more personal level.

CONCEPT BUILDINGS

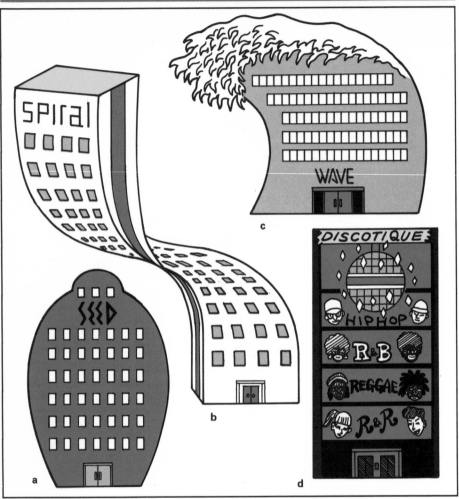

- Popular in Japan now are "theme buildings" catering to all the needs of carefully targeted consumer groups.

a   Seed is in Tokyo's Shibuya district. Each floor serves a different aspect of the customer's ideal life: from adventuring at a bazaar to a formal night out to office life and leisure time.

b   The Spiral Building in Aoyama is an art and exhibition space. A gallery spirals up three floors. The basement has a restaurant with a Caribbean theme. On the second floor are housewares and gifts, and on top an auditorium for fashion shows.

c   Wave is a music, film, and media building in Roppongi. Floors sell records and CDs in galleries outfitted

with banks of video monitors that dispense concert dates and music news. A basement theater shows foreign films.

d The Disco Building in Roppongi has nine discos, each with a different theme. If you don't like the Parisian room on the fourth floor, go up a flight to the Hollywood-style disco.

e Tokyu Hands is a do-it-yourself project and hobbies store in Shibuya, with over three hundred thousand items on twenty-four levels covering eight stories. Besides merchandise, it offers ongoing how-to classes and services like bookbinding and making neon signs. The store also does household repairs and remodeling.

communications communications communications
communications communications communications
communications communications communication
communications communications communication
communications communications communication
communications communications communication
communications communications communication
communications communications communication
communications communications communication
communications communications communication
communications communications communication
communications communications communication
communications communications communication
communications communications communication
communications communications communication
communications communications communication
communications communications communication
communications communications communication
communications communications communication
communications communications communication
communications communications communication
communications communications communication
communications communications communication
communications communications communication
communications communications communication
communications communications communication
communications communications communication

CHANGE MACHINES AND REAL-TIME MAPS

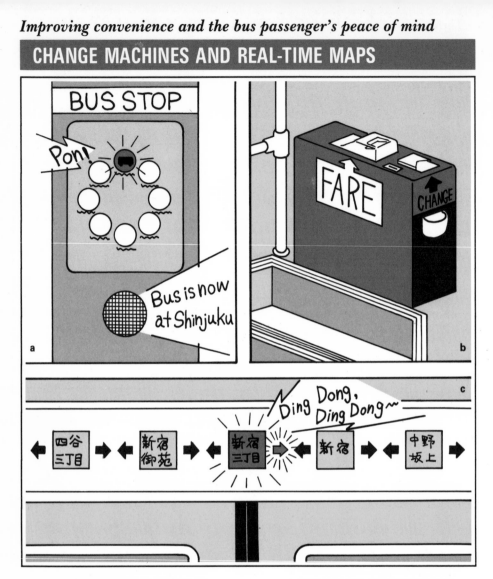

a At many bus stops, electronic locators tell exactly when the next bus due reaches the three stops prior to the stop you're waiting at. This eases the anxiety of waiting passengers, and helps them decide whether they should catch a cab or call ahead to tell their appointment they'll be late.

b Sophisticated change machines on buses can issue tickets and handle coins and paper money, as well as read magnetically encoded passes.

c In some subway cars, the direction the train is traveling in and the name of the next station are displayed on a map as the train is moving. This is helpful on crowded cars when the view out the window is blocked.

PUBLIC POLLUTION MONITORS

- In 1970 electronic-display pollution monitors were first installed in fifteen places in Tokyo to show noise levels and the percentages of carbon monoxide, sulfur oxide, and nitrogen oxide (the components of photochemical smog). The idea was to draw the public's attention to problems of the urban environment. Most monitors are in front of train stations and ward halls, places where people are likely to gather. When the pollution level gets too high, loudspeakers sound out warnings that advise young children and seniors to stay indoors. The monitors also double as newsboards for important public service announcements.

BUILDING CONVENTIONS

a Red triangles placed in specified windows of office buildings tell firefighters where a path inside and out is clear for entry during a fire. These passages must be kept clear while the building is in use. By law, buildings over three stories that lack exposed exterior stairways must have these marks on each floor.

b Construction sites of new houses and buildings are always wrapped head to toe in a frame covered with plastic or cloth. This cuts insurance liability by lowering the risk of falling objects hitting passersby. It also lowers visual, noise, and dust pollution and reduces antagonism with the neighbors.

VIDEO BILLBOARDS ON WHEELS

- Used frequently by Japanese liquor and cosmetics companies, Mobotron is a giant, wheeled VCR with a screen measuring ten by thirteen feet. It is rented by the day and will go wherever its clients desire. It can be driven through city streets as the video—with accompanying commercial soundtrack—plays, or it can be used in fixed locations, such as at a golf course, a classroom, a company sports event, or a convention. The leasing company helps plan Mobotron ad campaigns and will produce and edit videos to order. Rented by the day, Mobotron costs ¥1 million, slightly more on holidays. The price includes truck, driver, and gas.

UNIQUE TV SHOWS

a Celebrities enjoy culinary delights abroad. *TV Guide* says, "After visiting a town in Tunis where André Gide lived, they sample seafood at a restaurant aboard a ship."

b A reporter asks a young woman on the street if he can follow her home with his TV crew. At her apartment they go through her closets and be-

longings, and film her taking a bath.

c Short-segment dramas with historical and contemporary themes, and over 250 episodes. Explores issues like education and aging.

d Unusual rituals and tools from other countries are shown, while panelists try to guess what's going on. Part quiz show, part *National Geographic.*

e   Local talents perform regional songs and dances. Broadcasts originate from a different town each week, introducing Japanese subcultures.

f   Adult show originating alternately from Tokyo and Osaka. Discussions with guests are mixed with segments where the host introduces new sex clubs and sexual entertainments.

g   A desperate wife comes in with a story of how her husband left her. Viewers call in with tips. The TV crew stalks the man, finds him, and confronts him on camera.

h   Crazy sports event show: eating live frogs, sewing a button onto your tongue, drinking milk through your nose and expelling it from your eyes.

EFFECTIVE TV COMMERCIALS

a One technique for ramming the message home on Japanese TV is to show the exact same commercial twice in a row without pause. Such double-bite commercials are usually short, loud, dumb, and cheaply made, the equivalent of the American ads featuring real used car salesmen. The lamer the production, the more effective it becomes when shown twice.

b Ad agencies work closely with record and movie companies to ensure that TV commercials, concerts, and films are all released on a strategic schedule for maximum profit and exposure. Music credits are given on commercials. Record jackets often say, "As seen on the Honda ad!"

BUS AND SUBWAY ADVERTISING

a   On Japanese buses prerecorded tapes announce all stops. Local companies buy time on these tapes for ¥260,000 a year. The announcer reminds passengers that this is where they get off to reach such and such a store. The bus company uses the money to improve facilities for the disabled.

b   In subways, ceiling posters hang down across the width of the cars, back to back, spaced every few feet, blowing in the breeze and changing every other day. The sides of cars are covered in placards, changed every week. Stickers on the windows and ads on the handstraps change monthly. No escape.

127

TISSUE PAPER GIVEAWAYS

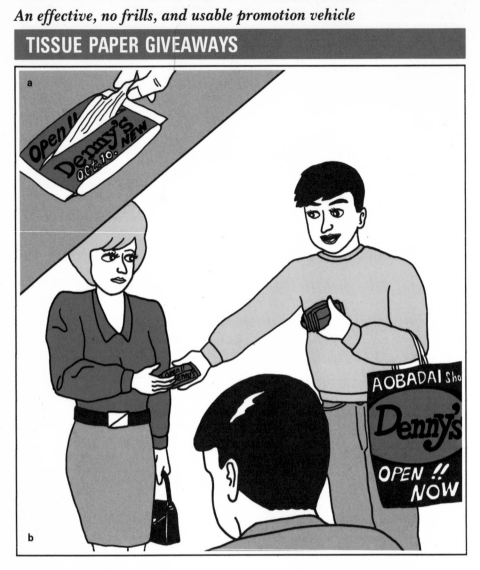

a What better way to get people to pay attention to you than to give them something that has your message on it, that is free and practical, and that they'll carry around with them and use often? The most common giveaway in Japan is packets of tissue paper. Why? Probably because most public restrooms in Japan still don't provide toilet paper and towels.

b Restaurant openings, bank promotions, and love hotel specials are occasions when employees stand on the street and hand packets of tissue to passersby. Note: While street leaflets in America are discarded as soon as they're passed out, tissues in Japan are held on to.

TRANSFERABLE DEBT PAYMENTS

- *Tegata* are short-term notes used by Japanese businesses to pay their debts. They represent secure debt in circulation outside normal financial centers, thus stimulating the economy. Unlike IOUs, the notes are guaranteed by an issuing bank, so their value is never in question. They come in terms of 60, 90, 120, 150, and 180 days. The payee can use the *tegata* to pay off his own debts by endorsing it over to another business, or he can take it to any bank and get an early redemption for cash at a 6 percent discount (the bank collects the full amount when the note is due). Companies paid by *tegata* will invoice at a 6 percent premium.

CORPORATE COMIC BOOKS

a   Some of Japan's largest and most blue-suited corporations—Mitsubishi Shoji, Hitachi, Fujitsu, Ricoh, Mitsui Bank—are now using comic book formats to speed and enhance the communication of information to their employees, customers, and stockholders. As the example here shows, a comic book panel (*left*) is far more effective than a photo (*right*) at setting a mood, and it offers more control over the image by allowing extraneous information to be removed.

b   Many Japanese in industry (both executives and workers) read comics as children and continue to read them as adults. Drawing styles, plots, and character types are well established

A young man is walking down the street minding his own business when suddenly a powerful car pulls up along side him driven by a somewhat dazzling and high-powered woman. She asks the young man, "Would you like a ride?" He says yes, but as he is about to get in, the car speeds away! The young man, his pride hurt, runs after the car but to no avail; the car is much too fast for him. Finally he falls down in the street totally exhausted. As if to add insult to injury the woman stops her car and tauntingly says to the young man, "Gee, it sure was fun. See you around!"

and quickly recognized. This makes it easier for corporate comic books to use cultural archetypes to target and communicate their messages. High educational standards and literacy rates enable comic books to address sophisticated modern-day problems without simplifying them.

c Pictured here is the same information communicated in comic book form and in narrative text. The comic is much more direct and engaging, and adds visual wit to an otherwise uneventful story. Annual reports (especially dismal ones), instruction manuals, and policy papers are just a few of the "serious" venues where comics are now used.

MAGAZINE AND COMIC BOOK CONCEPTS

a   A "serious" comic book that explains
    the Japanese economy, trade friction,
    the U.S. Federal Reserve system, and
    the Euroyen market, starring a young
    executive at a trading company and
    his S/M-loving boss. Features story of
    "Chrysly Motors" vs. "Toyosan."

b   A comic about traffic rules. Like many
    such informational comics, it uses a
    story line and not just illustrations to
    make the ideas easy to remember.

c   *Mono*, an international catalog-style
    magazine that each month focuses
    on a different class of objects:
    watches, stationery, kitchenware,
    etc. Includes prices and ordering info.

d   Comic book tale of a chef and the se-
    crets he learns on the road to

c **MONO** MAGAZINE

d COMICS **HOW TO COOK**

e **DISORDERS & PROBLEMS OF THE LIVER** COMICS

ABROAD MAGAZINE h

WOMEN's LAW ENCY-CLOPEDIA COMICS i

NIHONGO JOURNAL 京日本 あかさたなはまやらわん j

gourmet enlightenment. Contains recipes and cooking techniques.

e   Medical comics that present the basics of anatomy and disease.

f   Ideas of Marx, Freud, Einstein, etc. in narrative comic format.

g   Alvin Toffler's *The Third Wave* in comic format (two volumes).

h   A magazine compilation of ads for domestic and international packaged tours.

i   A comic book encyclopedia of women's law.

j   A monthly magazine for people studying Japanese, with articles on culture, usage, writing letters, pronunciation. Also versions for Chinese and Korean.

a   A book that explains different methods of burglary, murder, violent assault, fraud, and embezzlement.

b   A guidebook to public toilets, with photos, maps, and evaluations.

c   For the lecherous: A photo catalog of uniforms worn by young girls at schools around the city.

d   A guide to hot springs with photos of environs, lodgings, and meals served, in *mook*, or "magazine-book" format. *Mook* are sold on magazine racks at newsstands but contain book-length, illustrated discussions of fashion, cooking, crafts, current events, etc., all prepared by an editorial team.

e.   A series of books published once a week on no particular subject. Each is

around two hundred pages, paperback, with an eye-catching cover. Many are "concept books" by famous illustrators, musicians, and copywriters, who present their views on various subjects. One artist created a giant double-sided flip book.

f   A book that lists the prices of important commodities and services, such as how much to tip a nurse (done in Japan), how much to pay your marriage matchmaker, how much to pay in congratulations for a hole-in-one.

g   A children's book on bodily functions, featuring elephants, snakes, whales, and other animals (including people), with the message "Everybody eats, so everybody poops."

TEACHING BASIC VALUES

- Japanese schoolkids from elementary school through high school are expected to clean their own classrooms. They clean everything except ceilings and high windows, and in the process are taught how to create a "clean, sanitary, and beautiful environment as a basis for life." They also learn responsibility and how to work together as a group. Some schools have the children fast one day a week as a sign of appreciation for the food they have. Children wear uniforms, which make it difficult for the more affluent to show off fancy clothes. Teaching is a respectable profession in Japan and commands a higher salary than in the U.S.

PREVENTING AUTO ACCIDENTS

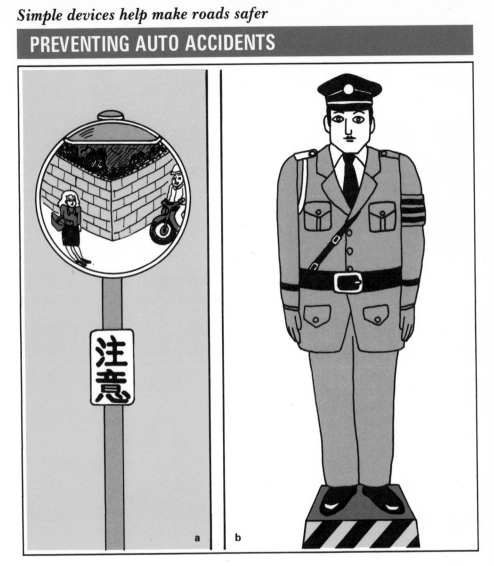

a   Freestanding or mounted on utility poles, convex mirrors are used at blind corners, on narrow streets, and at dangerous crossings to allow oncoming traffic and pedestrians to see what's approaching from the other side. In Meguro-ku, one of Tokyo's twenty-three wards, there are 1,600 such mirrors.

b   Two-dimensional, painted metal policemen are installed in busy intersections or on the shoulders of highways to get people to slow down and take care. They are also used in special campaigns against speeders and drunks. The metal figures are cheaper than real cops, and, psychologically, they work.

Mini–police stations for security, convenience, and good PR

POLICE BOXES

- Located throughout Japanese cities and towns are small hutlike structures called *koban*. All day, every day, police personnel stand guard here, keeping an eye out on the neighborhood, answering questions, and otherwise helping those in need of police services. At least two people are assigned to each box. One remains in the box as the other patrols the local streets on bicycle. In this way the neighborhood and the police get to know each other. The constant police presence and the familiarity of the police with what's happening on the streets helps reduce crime. Most *koban* also post the nationwide toll of the day's traffic accidents.

communications **138**

"NO SHOES INDOORS" SYSTEM

a   Japanese distinguish between inside and outside the home. Inside the entryway to all homes (and some restaurants) is an area for removing shoes. You then step up into the living area, wearing house slippers or in your stocking feet. (Slippers are never worn on the delicate surface of tatami, however.) Shoes are put on again only when it is time to leave. Taking shoes off keeps the house clean, is relaxing, and increases the amount of usable space, since you can sit on the floor without worrying about getting dirty.

b   The toilet is one area within the house considered "dirty," so separate slippers are provided there.

TELEPHONE AIDS FOR THE DISABLED

a   The *Onegai Techo* ("Do-me-a-favor Book") has a distinctive orange color, and on every page is printed, "I'm very sorry to bother you, but I'm deaf. Can you please make a telephone call for me?" A deaf person writes a message on a page and gives the book to a passerby, who makes the call and delivers the message. The book is provided free by NTT, the phone company.

b   Other phones for the disabled are a dialless phone with a blow tube, a phone that can be dialed by foot or elbow, a phone that flashes instead of ringing, a phone with special low-frequency bells. All phones have a raised 5 button to help the blind.

communications   **140**

MAKING CITIES SAFER FOR THE BLIND

a   Throughout Japanese cities, specially textured paving blocks embedded in sidewalks and concrete guide blind pedestrians along a safe route. A change in texture—to lateral bars, lengthwise bars, knobs, etc.—indicates a change in direction, stairs, or obstructions ahead. The blocks are most conspicuous at train stations, where they mark the edge of the platform—helps sighted people, too.

b   At major intersections, pushing a button will cause music to play out of loudspeakers at either end of the crosswalk when the light turns green. This helps the blind hone in on their destination, and also tells them when it's safe to cross.

MESSAGE AND INFORMATION CENTERS

a

a   One way to bring customers to your store is to make it into a space that offers more than just the lure of consumerism. Shopping malls in the United States have taken over the old function of downtown as a place to meet. A similar phenomenon can be seen in crowded Japanese cities, where interactive computers are helping turn department stores into "central message stations." Using these on-site electronic bulletin boards, anyone can come in and leave a message for friends. This is especially useful in case of a sudden change of plans or as a regular drop box for one's particular group of urban playmates. At the entrance to

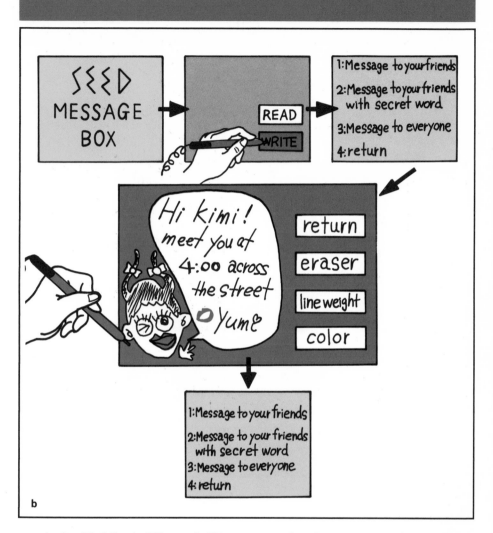

b

the Seed Building in Shibuya, six TV monitors sit atop a console called the Seed Message Box.

b At the Box, there are two user-friendly computer message stations, each with a light pen and menus. Just respond to the series of options the computer gives you. You can read a message from your friend, respond to it, or leave a new one, for your friend or for the world to see. Press a button and get a color printout. All for free. Located strategically near the entrances to many department stores are also coffee shops, passages to underground malls, small-scale exhibitions, event spaces, lottery booths, and other come-ons.

MAGAZINE HOUSE

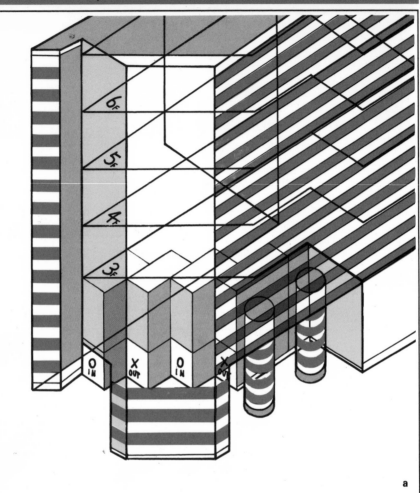

a

a   This is the Tokyo headquarters of Magazine House, publisher of the trendy magazines *Brutus* (like *Esquire*, with articles about style, neat things, lifestyles, and famous people), *Popeye* (like *Brutus*, but for younger men), *Olive* (like *Popeye*, but for women), *An An* (a fashion magazine), and *Tarzan* (health, fitness, and fashion for men). The company wanted a headquarters as hip as its magazines. The building is designed as a small town, with each magazine editorial office functioning as a separate "neighborhood." The ground floor coffee shop, library, and TV are the town squares. On the eighth floor is a roof garden for relaxing.

b   The building's silver and pink stripes were designed to stand out in the crowd of buildings nearby.

c   The emphasis in the public spaces is on information. People can watch a twenty-four-hour live hook-up with CNN news or view performance and video artists on a bank of monitors.

d   The World Magazine Gallery stocks just about every important magazine, large and small, from around the world. Magazines are arranged by country. Anyone is welcome to come in and browse. A photocopy machine is available, and you cam take the magazines to the coffee shop next door to enjoy with a giant slice of chocolate cake.

PUBLIC GATHERING PLACES

a   Sony Plaza was built in the mid-1970s as Japan's first showroom building. Located on the Ginza, it is a natural gathering place for passersby. Sony has spared no effort to scream the corporate identity into the public's collective consciousness. Outside, an event space is rented out on a daily or weekly basis to different organizations, who use it to promote their products and causes.

b   Inside are banks of TV monitors and a room of Sony products and listening compartments. There are also coffee shops, boutiques, and a stairway where each step sounds a different musical note. The basement has an American drugstore.

TAKING CORPORATE RESPONSIBILITY

- After a 1982 Japan Air Lines crash, the company president visited the victims in the hospital and their family members, presenting a gift of cash. In 1987 JAL's president attended a memorial service for 520 people killed in a crash the year before, and all employees observed a period of silence and prayer. When things go wrong, it is usually up to the company president in Japan to assume responsibility, regardless of where the fault actually lies. This shows sincerity and the desire to make amends. Far from increasing liability, such corporate blame-taking actually reduces claims. And maybe the bosses sleep better at night.

SUGGESTION BOXES

- Nobody knows what's wrong with an assembly process or a warehousing system better than the people who use it. Japanese companies make a point of soliciting—and rewarding—suggestions on how to improve operations from employees. The Nissan Motor factory in Zama, for example, rewards each and every idea sug-gested, from ¥100 to ¥3 million, depending upon its value when adopted. Japanese workers overall make an average of 24 suggestions to their companies per year, ten times the rate in the U.S. At Canon, there are 443 suggestions per employee, which have added up to a savings of ¥50.5 million per worker.

The All-Honda Idea Contest: *making dreams come true*

a

b

c

- Every other year in the fall Honda holds a contest where employees use company money to develop ideas for new vehicles and transportation concepts. Practicality is not necessarily a criterion for success. Recently, 6,000 proposals were received, but only 179 were picked for the semifinals. The contest, held at an amusement park, offered prizes in three categories: engine, free, and specified (e.g., speed). Among the submissions:

a Surprise Roller: motorized skates.

b Parent and Child Automobile: good for getting around the neighborhood.

c 3-D Mobility Vehicle: allows you to cruise on the highway and rise up to see traffic and obstructions ahead.

appendix appendix appendix appendix appendix
appendix appendix appendix appendix appendix
appendix appendix appendix appendix appendix
appendix appendix appendix appendix appendix
appendix appendix appendix appendix appendix
appendix appendix appendix appendix appendix
appendix appendix appendix appendix appendix
appendix appendix appendix appendix appendix
appendix appendix appendix appendix appendix
appendix appendix appendix appendix appendix
appendix appendix appendix appendix appendix
appendix appendix appendix appendix appendix
appendix appendix appendix appendix appendix
appendix appendix appendix appendix appendix
appendix appendix appendix appendix appendix
appendix appendix appendix appendix appendix
appendix appendix appendix appendix appendix
appendix appendix appendix appendix appendix
appendix appendix appendix appendix appendix
appendix appendix appendix appendix appendix
appendix appendix appendix appendix appendix
appendix appendix appendix appendix appendix
appendix appendix appendix appendix appendix
appendix appendix appendix appendix appendix
appendix appendix appendix appendix appendix
appendix appendix appendix appendix appendix
appendix appendix appendix appendix appendix

page 14/Capsule office building

Built in 1972, the Nakagin Building is considered one of architect Kisho Kurokawa's most important works. He still has his office here. Units were originally priced at $25,000 (1.5 times the average at the time) and sold out quickly. The modular design inspired the "capsule bed," ten million of which have been sold to date. Each bed unit contains a TV, alarm clock, emergency button, and radio—in addition to a mattress. Nakagin Capsule Tower Building, c/o Nakagin Housing Inc., Nakagin Honsha Building 6F, 8-16-10 Ginza, Chuo-ku, Tokyo 104 (03-545-9211).

page 16/Urine and hot oil solidifiers

Urea Pot is made by Smith Inc., 2-8-5 Iwamoto-cho, Chiyoda-ku, Tokyo 101 (03-864-7641), and sells for ¥300 in drug stores, supermarkets, and gas stations. Katameru Tempuru is by Johnson Inc., 699 Hongo Kokufu, Oiso-cho, Kanagawa 259 (0463-72-2111). A related product is Fashionable Cat. This is a safe chemical added to your cat's food or drink so that its urine won't smell.

page 17/Stylish five- and six-door refrigerators

Another useful feature of these refrigerators is that you can redesign whole compartments to meet your storage needs.

They come with lots of trays, baskets, and drawers to create micro-microzones. Most large appliance makers sell these models. The particular one described here is by Sharp Inc., Yawata-cho 8, Ichigaya, Shinjuku-ku, Tokyo 162 (03-260-1161).

pages 18–19/New food concoctions

Weird ice creams by Donatello's Japan Inc., Sugitaya Building 2F, 1-4-20 Yaesu, Chuo-ku, Tokyo 103 (03-273-1083). For Joan Restaurant in Shinjuku, call 03-356-5285. Here's a guide to "mixed beer" cocktails you can get in Tokyo: "Dog's Nose" is beer and gin. "Mint Beer" is beer and mint liqueur. "Red Eye" is beer and tomato juice. "Beer Buster" is beer and vodka. "Panache" is beer and lemon juice. "White Velvet" is beer and champagne. In Japanese, read *Oyatsu Story* ("Snack Story"; published by Kodansha), which gives the background to odd Japanese concoctions like spicy caviar candy and mustard chewing gum.

page 20/Designer fruit

Watermelons by Tokyo Chuo Seika (03-544-7663). For designer apples, contact the Abe Farm, 13 Aza Inamura, Oaza Namioka, Namioka-cho, Aomori 038 (0172-62-2141). Price range is ¥600–1,200 in made-to-order lots of 200. Square apples are also available. For information call Hiroka Inc., 1-2 Aza Iwai, Oaza

Takasaki, Hirosaki, Aomori 036 (0172-27-5511). The inventor of the inscribed apple technique is Hakuo Iwasaki (0172-34-4545). For ¥90,000 he will grow an apple in a bottle that will last two months.

page 21/Head-cooling pillows

Electric cooling pillows by Hitachi Inc., 2-15-12 Nishi Shinbashi, Minato-ku, Tokyo 105 (03-502-2111). One brand of plastic-cylinder pillow is called the Hyma Pillow. It measures twelve by twenty inches and costs ¥5,000. By Hakuyosha Inc., 2-11-1 Shimomaruko, Ota-ku, Tokyo 146 (03-756-1111). Cheaper models by other makers begin at ¥1,800.

page 23/Anti–obscene-phone-call machine

For Sony, contact 6-7-35 Kita Shinagawa, Shinagawa-ku, Tokyo 141 (03-448-2111). Another privacy protector is Sanyo's Selectaphone. A prerecorded voice asks a caller to press the secret code. Only callers who correctly press the code buttons are allowed to ring through. You can also punch in all the numbers you want to receive. Others are rejected. Numbers that do ring through are displayed on an LCD screen for a minute so that you can preview them. If you don't pick up the phone, the caller is disconnected. The Selectaphone stores up to thirty numbers and has two melodies for hold. Contact Sanyo Denki Inc.,

Domestic Sales Dept., 100 Higashi-cho, Onichi-higashi-cho, Moriguchi, Osaka 570 (06-901-1111).

page 24/Sing-along machines

Instead of a digital readout, some *karaoke* players reward your efforts with one, two, or three trumpet fanfares at the end of the song. Models described here are made by Clarion Tokyo Hanbai Inc., 1-15-20 Yoga, Setagaya-ku, Tokyo 158 (03-707-2511). Price range ¥59,000–200,000. For professional units, contact Fuji Lease, 2-13-15 Ebisu-nishi, Shibuya-ku, Tokyo 150 (03-496-6121). Another machine records performances from TV, radio, and records and then reduces the vocal track by 90 percent to produce a custom *karaoke* tape; contact Matsushita Denki Sangyo Inc., 1-1-2 Shibakoen, Minato-ku, Tokyo 105 (03-437-1121). Sony's Personal Karaoke Practice Machine ANK-L2 is the same size as a Walkman and comes with a microphone hooked into the headphone. Contact Sony Inc., 6-7-35 Kita Shinagawa, Shinagawa-ku, Tokyo 141 (03-448-2111).

page 25/Cozy table/desk

A standard item in most Japanese houses, electric *kotatsu* are made by every major Japanese appliance maker. Price range ¥10,000–100,000 depending on design, materials, and size. The tables are usually square, but rounds and rectangles are also available. Users sit on the floor, but leg extenders can be purchased to boost the height in summer, when heating is unnecessary. Toshiba's model KY-136DFC has a microprocessor that senses the room temperature and adjusts the *kotatsu*'s heat level accordingly. The cozy *kotatsu* experience is enhanced when it is placed on a thermostatically controlled heated carpet, also available from Toshiba Inc., Heating Equipment Sales Dept., 24 C Zone, Toshiba Building, 1-1-1 Shibaura, Minato-ku, Tokyo 105 (03-457-3684).

page 26/Sensor-controlled mirrors

The full name of the system is Taiyoko Saiko System Natulight. Made by Tecnet Inc. (Technology Network), Yoshizawa Building, 2-17-7 Kyobashi, Chuo-ku, Tokyo 104 (03-535-4111). Another way to solve the problem of sunlight is offered by Misawa Homes, which makes houses that turn 180 degrees over the course of a day so that each room gets a little sun. A three-story, 2,300-square-foot home (not including land) costs ¥25 million.

page 27/Home double-decker garage

Manufactured by Matsushita Denko, 1048 Kadoma, Kadoma City, Osaka 571. In Tokyo call 03-454-6111.

pages 28–29/Automated prefab downtown parking tower

Mitsubishi Heavy Industry Inc., Three Dimensional Parking Department, 2-5-1 Marunouchi, Chiyoda-ku, Tokyo 100 (03-212-3111), assembles components purchased from other companies and uses a local crew to dig the foundation.

page 30/Retractable carwash

Manufactured by Yasui Inc., 1-2 Higashi Shinbashi, Minato-ku, Tokyo 105 (03-574-0561).

page 31/Washing machine cleaning enhancers

Zabu Zabu Balls by Sanai Inc., 4163 Nakafuji, Kuramurayama, Tokyo 190 (0424-60-7738). These and other handy laundry products are distributed by Daiya (03-384-6131).

pages 32–33/Creative housewares

The ironing board is a product of Seibu's Shufunome ("Housewife's Brand") line of housewares. These housewares are developed using laboratory testing and the reports of four thousand housewife monitors who try new products and offer their opinions on how they can be improved. Some products developed by the Shufunome people are clothespins that don't leave marks on clothing, devices to mix bath water (useful for Japanese baths, which when left standing become very hot near the surface and very cold near the bottom of the tub), and dish drainers set a little bit higher than normal to improve air circulation and inhibit mold. Contact Seibu Department Stores, Sunshine 60, 3-1-1 Higashi Ikebukuro, Toshima-ku, Tokyo 170 (03-989-0111).

page 34/Combination toilet-sink

The toilet-sink is by Toto Kiki Inc., 2-1-1 Nakajima, Kokurakita-ku, Kitakyushu, Fukuoka 802 (in Tokyo, 03-595-9736). The flush-sound device is by Shonan Automation, 136 Kawai Honcho, Asahi-ku, Yokohama, Kanagawa 241 (045-953-5093).

page 35/Toilet for hemorrhoid sufferers

Demonstration and ordering at Toto Tokyo Showroom, Toto Pavilion, 7-8-7 Ginza, Chuo-ku, Tokyo 104 (03-573-1010). Soon to come on the market—the product of a joint venture by Toto, NTT (the telephone company), and Tateishi Electric—is the "Intelligent Toilet," which uses built-in seat sensors to analyze blood pressure, urine, pulse, and weight. Digital analysis of body waste is instantly shown on an attached liquid-crystal display.

page 36/Accessories for the Japanese bath

Almost all Japanese bath accessories are available in three coordinated colors (pastel pink, baby blue, and light green) at supermarkets. The slippers cost ¥580. Tub covers are ¥2,600–6,800. Water pumps are ¥1,800–8,000 and move twelve to sixteen liters per minute. Contact Terada Pump Seisakujo, 3-17 Shinonome-cho, Yamato Takada, Nara 635 (0745-52-5101).

page 37/Hot springs water delivery service

For delivery of hot springs water by tank truck, call Odakyu Department Store, 1-1-3 Nishi Shinjuku, Shinjuku-ku, Tokyo 160 (03-342-1111). The water comes from Iwaku hot spring in Minami Nasu, Tochigi Prefecture, several hours north of Tokyo. Price of a bathtub full (200 liters) including delivery is ¥5,800. To order from the Kowakien Inn at Hakone contact Mr. Morimoto at 1297 Ninotaira, Hakone-machi, Ashigarashimo-gun, Kanagawa 250 (0460-2-4111). The water is good for the skin, stomach, and nervous system. Cost is ¥1,500 for 20 liters plus ¥700–900 for shipping anywhere in Japan. Or buy packets of Nippon no Meito, which contain formulations of the mineral compositions of water at hot springs throughout Japan. Each is for a different ailment: arthritis, aching joints and muscles, skin disease, nervous distress, fatigue, hemorrhoids. Cost is ¥120 for 30 grams (good for one bath). Made by Tsumurajuntendo Inc., 12-7 Niban-cho, Chiyoda-ku, Tokyo 102 (03-221-0001).

page 38/Instant rejuvenation aids

Cool Band for ¥14,800 by Hitachi Kaden Hanbai, 2-15-12 Nishi Shinbashi, Minato-ku, Tokyo 105 (03-502-2111). Another model by Magima Co. plugs into the car cigarette lighter and reduces the risk of accident by preventing drowsiness while driving. Estoron King and Youthgen King are from S. S. Seiyaku Inc., 2-12-4 Hamacho, Nihonbashi, Chuo-ku, Tokyo 103 (03-668-4511). There are also coffee shops and bars that dispense pure oxygen to revive less-than-alert customers. The Miden coffee shop in Osaka offers ten minutes with an oxygen mask for ¥850. The Shochu Kyowakoku bar in Shibuya, Tokyo, lets inebriated customers spend five minutes in their oxygen chamber for ¥100.

page 39/Belly bands, face masks, and stress gum

Stomach warmers cost about ¥800 and are sold at most pharmacies and department stores. Face masks cost ¥100 and are made by numerous companies, among them Sakae Hope Inc., 4-1-28 Kikawa-nishi, Yodogawa-ku, Osaka 532 (06-306-1081). Stress-age Gum comes six to a pack for ¥80 and is made by S. B. Shokuhin Inc., 18-6 Kabuto-cho, Nihonbashi, Chuo-ku, Tokyo 103 (03-668-0551).

pages 40–41/A few more zany ideas

Radicame by Yonezawa Co., 3-16-6 Asa-kusabashi, Taito-ku, Tokyo 111 (03-861-6361). Cost of the Buddhist altar is ¥50,000 for the tape unit, ¥70,000 for the CD version. Call Sanrei Inc., 3-2-8 Kamitomino, Kokurakita-ku, Kitakyushu, Fukuoka 802 (093-551-3030). Team Demi kits come in eight colors and are made by Plus Corp., 1-20-11 Otowa, Bunkyo-ku, Tokyo (03-942-3090). Popping ice is by Nihon Gokan (03-212-7111).

pages 44–45/Full-service taxis

Kusaka Taxi in Tokyo offers maximum service. The driver has beer, candy, and cigarettes for sale, and the cab comes with TV, video, the ever-present sing-along machine, and an electric frying pan. You can make arrangements for early morning pick-up, and the driver will give you a wake-up call. Cost? The same as a regular cab. Call Mr. Kusaka at 03-312-0314.

pages 46–47/Household moving services

Offered by Art Hikkoshi Center, 2-485-1 Izumi-cho, Daito, Osaka 574 (0720-75-0123). The company is run by an ex-housewife, whose goal is to offer services that women will appreciate, since the women in Japan often plan and organize household moves.

page 48/Drive-home service

Working hours are 7 P.M. to 4 A.M. Cost is

¥1,000 for the first two kilometers, plus ¥90 for every five hundred meters after that. Very reasonable, considering that two escorts are needed. One company offering this service is Nishi Nippon Unten Daiko, 2123-1 Higashi Kushihara-cho, Kurume, Fukuoka 830 (0942-32-1710). An association of similar companies is the Zenkoku Unten Daiko Rengo Kyokai (0924-74-0010).

page 49/Airport and department store courtesy staff

Courtesy staff jobs are almost always held by young, unmarried women. The pay is bad, but advancement is a possibility, and knowing how to speak well and handle customers' needs is a distinct advantage in Japan. Training in speech, posture, and mannerisms is rigorous, because customers demand it and because politeness and decorum create a mood of harmony, comfort, and respectability. For information on courtesy service personnel, contact Miss Kotani at Hankyu Department Store (03-575-2062) or Mr. Iwai at Takashimaya Department Store (03-211-4111).

page 50/Eliminating bank lines

A useful service Japanese banks offer is paying your monthly bills for you automatically: phone, gas, electric, rent, public TV, credit cards. For a small fee, the bank will also deposit funds in any account in Japan you specify. This is the most common way of paying bills in Japan, since few Japanese have checking accounts. Every day, city banks send tellers around to nearby office buildings to service business accounts and individual depositors—this makes it possible for many office workers to do all their banking without ever going to the bank (always crowded at lunch hour). Banks also send their clerks around to depositors' homes at New Year's to offer greetings and try to win new business. For information on banking services in Japan, contact Kyowa Bank, 1-1-2 Otemachi, Chiyoda-ku, Tokyo 100 (03-287-2111), or Sumitomo Bank, 1-3-2 Marunouchi, Chiyoda-ku, Tokyo 100 (03-282-5084).

page 51/Land trusts

Mitsui Bank has eighteen branches that deal in real estate in Tokyo and thirty-seven more in other parts of Japan. Like other banks, Mitsui has a network of related companies under its corporate umbrella—construction companies, management firms, real estate agencies—all of which make it possible to keep 100 percent of the profits and the work in the same family. For more information, contact Mitsui Bank, 2-1-1 Muromachi, Nihonbashi, Chuo-ku, Tokyo 103 (03-270-9511).

page 52/Handyman agencies

Seishin Service in Tokyo has six full-time

and seventy part-time employees, who include college professors, lawyers, accountants, and people from all walks of life with almost every imaginable expertise. Contact 4-16-12 Higashi Nakano, Nakano-ku, Tokyo 164 (03-362-0606).

page 53/Hairstyle pre-imaging and scalp massages

Hair Simulator is made by E.R.C. Inc., 1-9-22 Higashi Zakura, Higashi-ku, Nagoya, Aichi 461 (052-962-4091). Contact Mr. Hayashida. Costs ¥2.6 million to purchase, or rents for ¥50,000 per month.

Page 54/Food service amenities

Many companies make ultrarealistic plastic food samples. One is Keiei Shokuhin Sample Seisakusho, 1-21-1 Takada, Toshima-ku, Tokyo 171 (03-983-7384). In summer, o-shibori are kept in a "hot box" at the restaurant so they are always ready for use. The cloths, in sanitary plastic wrappers, are provided by regular cleaning and delivery services. One such company is Meiko Raburin, 3-6-5 Kita Shinagawa, Shinagawa-ku, Tokyo 140 (03-471-1225). For ¥9,000 they supply restaurants with a minimum of 1,300 clean, moist towels and charge ¥5 for each additional one. For home use, Matsushita Electric sells the Hot Towel Mini for ¥5,000. Put folded towels inside and water in the base, and in twenty minutes you have four ready-to-wipe

o-shibori. Contact Matsushita Denki Sangyo Inc., 1-1-2 Shibakoen, Minato-ku, Tokyo 105 (03-437-1121).

page 55/Home food delivery in real dishes

Home food delivery is called demae. Generally, you can get sushi, tempura, Chinese food, noodles, and—now— Domino's pizza (albeit in a cardboard box). Neighborhood restaurants in cities generally don't deliver more than a mile or so away from the kitchen. Insulated hot boxes that keep food from spilling are made by many companies, including Ebisu Menki, 2-6-30 Ebisu, Shibuya-ku, Tokyo 150 (03-446-1610).

pages 56–57/Coffee shop concepts

There are over one hundred twenty thousand coffee shops in Japan. Kabutocho (044-63-6886) is named after Japan's equivalent of Wall Street, where the stock exchange is located. In Tokyo try Hayase, with a fortune teller on weekdays (except Tuesday) from 9 A.M. (03-352-1900); Boronte, with various palmists and physiognomists to read hands and heads (03-354-7550); Jupiter, where the chairs all hang from ropes so that you can swing in them (03-710-5290); Cabin, which looks like the cabin of a ship and has a bell sounding watch every half-hour (03-920-7865); Saikai, shaped like a bank complete with 3,400 safe deposit boxes (03-667-0054, the

owner worked for a securities firm);
Buruju, a sexy lingerie shop where items
can be tried on in a dressing room (03-
382-2641).

page 58/Tiny bars

There is not a big profit in running a tiny
bar, but if your personality appeals to
the right number of people you can
make a decent living (especially considering the outrageous markup on whiskey, which most customers accept will-
ingly in return for a place to sit and
while away the evening hours). Obtain-
ing a liquor license in Japan is fairly
easy. There are many gay bars in the
larger cities—although half the clientele
may be straight. Generally Japanese
men have several "favorite bars" scat-
tered around the city. Here they are
known and can expect a warm greeting
whenever they go in, even though their
visits might be several months apart. At
some bars, patrons share particular in-
terests, like baseball, golf, or haiku.
These small living rooms do much to re-
lieve the anonymity of the big city and
are good places for Japanese people to
belong to groups outside of their normal
company and neighborhood affiliations.

page 59/Bottle keep and endless appetizers

So-called "keep bars" are in every city
throughout Japan. Sake bars will keep
bottles of premium sake on hand, too.

One much-appreciated gesture is to tell
a friend you know is going to one of
your favorite parts of town to drop by
your regular bar there and have a drink
from your personal store. A system just
getting under way in Japan is a computerized "keep" system that ties together an association of bars all over
Japan. You take your membership card
to a new bar in a different city and present it to the bartender. The amount of
whiskey you drink is then automatically
deducted from your bottle back home.
New variant: There are now "keep bottles" for expensive types of seaweed at
a few Japanese restaurants.

pages 60–61/Capsule hotels

In the Shinbashi area of Tokyo, try
staying at Capsule Hotel Business,
4-12-11 Shinbashi, Minato-ku, Tokyo 105
(03-431-1391), only three minutes from
the station. Cost is ¥3,800 a night. Capsule units are made by Kotobuki Inc.,
1-2-12 Yurakucho, Chiyoda-ku, Tokyo 100
(03-591-1311). They make four kinds of
capsules, differing primarily by the loca-
tion of the entrance. The company has
been making capsules since 1979 and
has sold over twelve thousand to date.
The price of ¥700,000–850,000 includes
installation. You can order one at a time
(for a spare room at home, say, or for a
temporary dormlike set-up on an isolated work site).

page 62/Coin sneaker laundry

Manufactured by Sanyo Electric, 1-1-10 Ueno, Taito-ku, Tokyo 110 (03-835-1111). The washer/dryer set costs ¥300,000. Sanyo will give laundromat owners a loan toward purchase. The company estimates each cycle costs ¥31 for the washer and ¥11 for the dryer. Customers pay ¥200 and ¥100 respectively. Used three times a day, the washer/dryer will be paid off in a year.

page 63/Safety-box underwear laundry

Men's Clean Koenji is at 4-17-12 Koenji-kita, Suginami-ku, Tokyo 166 (03-310-4221).

pages 64–65/Community public baths

Baths are usually open from mid-afternoon to 10 P.M. or midnight. They are closed once a week for cleaning; vacation days are staggered among the local baths so a bath is always open nearby. Since more and more Japanese have baths in their homes, the public baths are having financial troubles. But they are still the mainstay of college students who live in tiny apartments with no amenities and old men who go to socialize and get out of the house. Some baths have installed laundromats to generate extra income; clean your clothes and body at the same time. A new development is twenty-four-hour coin-op shower rooms, so you can bathe any time of the day or night. For more information, contact the bathhouse association, Honda Yokujo Kumiai, at 03-692-4707 in Tokyo.

page 66/Paper-recycling truck

For information about this service and how it works, contact Mr. Kishi, Shigen Kaishu Jigyo Kyodo Kumiai, 2-21-1 Masaki-cho, Chiyoda-ku, Tokyo 101 (03-263-3676).

page 67/Telephone services for busy people

There are many other services available by phone. One company offers telephone English lessons for executives who don't have time to attend school. Another helps you plan your dates: You tell them how much you want to spend and what kind of evening you want to have, and they will advise you of restaurants, places to go for walks, entertainments. The bill comes later. Tel Information Japan's Yellow Telephone service (03-353-9171) gives you citywide information. For example, you ask them where in the Harajuku area you can find an English-language class for engineering students, and they will track it down while you're still on the line.

page 68/Cosmetic surgery to improve your life

Surgery at the Jujin Clinic is generally

performed on an outpatient basis, but you can elect a three-day hospitalization at about ¥40,000. Some 15 percent of the clinic's patients are male college graduates trying to improve their appearance and thus improve their chances of being hired by big companies. Usually they ask the doctors at Jujin to fix their noses or make their eyelids more "Western looking." Contact Jujin Clinic, 1-4-5 Shinbashi, Minato-ku, Tokyo 105 (03-571-2111).

page 69/Automobile body cloning

Eva Inc., 2-5-7 Kirigaoka, Midori-ku, Yokohama, Kanagawa 227 (045-922-1321). The company says it has received permission from Corvette and Mazda to make their clone kits. For Mad House garage, contact 0550-75-3368 in Shizuoka Prefecture.

page 73/Restaurant promotions

Call Ribera in Tokyo at 03-446-6941. Dairy Chiko is in the Nakano section of Tokyo (03-386-4461). Call Otoya in Osaka at 06-985-6134. At Marutani in Tokyo (03-672-0041) eat a hundred gyoza (pot stickers) in seventy minutes and get them for free.

page 74/Sadistic cuisines

A restaurant featuring the Cruel Cuisine is Yacht, 1161-6 Hamashima-cho, Shima, Mie 517 (0599-53-0486). Serving tofu with dojo is Okutan in Kyoto (075-561-6969) and Tofuya in Tokyo (03-582-1028).

page 75/Catch-as-catch-can cuisine

Two Kyoto restaurants featuring nagashi somen are Beniya (075-741-2041) and Nakayoshi (075-741-2081).

page 76/One ingredient, multicourse restaurants

A restaurant serving bamboo cuisine is Kinsuitei, at 2-15-15 Tenjin, Nagaokakyo, Kyoto 617 (075-951-5151). Kinsuitei is located in an area noted for its fine bamboo growths, and serves this cuisine only in April and May, when the bamboo is freshest. Another favorite "single ingredient" is tofu. A tofu meal with five or seven courses costs ¥3,000 or more per person and features fried tofu skin, grilled tofu, tofu sheet soup, tofu bran and vegetables, deep fried tofu balls, cold tofu with ginger and scallions, and so on. Other featured ingredients at restaurants are fugu (blow fish), red sea bream, organically grown chickens, and whale.

page 77/Cook-it-yourself restaurants

Okonomiyaki means "grill as you like it." Restaurants specializing in this dish cater to a youthful low-budget crowd. Low grill tables are placed in rows and surrounded by comfortable cushions for sitting. You are encouraged to drink beer as you wait for the grill to warm up. Try Taruya, 2-20-6 Dogenzaka, Shibuya-ku, Tokyo (03-461-3325). *Nabemono* restaurants are slightly more upscale and are a good place to enjoy conversation with friends and family. The cuisine is extremely healthy, featuring vegetables, tofu, fish, and chicken. In the variety known as *shabu shabu*, thinly sliced pieces of lean beef are parboiled in the simmering pot and then dipped in raw egg. Try Furiwake, 3-35-13 Yushima, Bunkyo-ku, Tokyo (03-836-5888), for a special kind of *nabemono* fed to sumo wrestlers to make them gain weight.

page 78/Rental restaurants

Grand Chef is in the Yugen Building 3F, 6-3-17 Ginza, Chuo-ku, Tokyo 104 (03-572-2527), and is rented out almost every day.

page 79/Rooftop beer gardens

Beer gardens are generally open May to September from 5 to 10 P.M. At any major hub in a city you are sure to find several; listings can also be found on teleguide services throughout the city. Prices are moderate. At one, for example, you get all you can eat and drink in two hours, including tax, for ¥3,300. By day, many of the same department store rooftops serve as amusement areas for children, with small rides and games.

For more information you can contact Buriyan Beer Terrace, Shinyurakucho Building 12F, 1-12-1 Yurakucho, Chiyoda-ku, Tokyo 100 (03-216-4621).

page 81/Theme train cars

The cost of Joyful Cars is the same as for a reserved, first-class ticket. JR also runs something akin to a "magical mystery tour" day train for children. It goes nowhere in particular, arriving where it left after a few hours of fun. Some of the cars are open plan, with no seats and with walls decorated with kids' favorite cartoon characters. While in transit, a play director leads the children in versions of treasure hunt, hide-and-go-seek, and other games. Some cars have child-size carpets, tables, and chairs for relaxing. Cost of a day for kids is ¥4,980, for adults ¥6,950. Contact the Japan Railways PR corner at 03-212-3583 and see the *Joyful Train Book* published by Japan Travel Bureau (03-284-7502).

pages 84–85/Vending machines

Near some of the video rental machines is a preview machine showing five-second clips from hundreds of artists. Nakayama Inc., 2-12-8 Shinjuku, Shinjuku-ku, Tokyo 160 (03-352-7181), makes electronic vending machines, specializing in ticket vendors, change machines, magazine machines, and machines that use cards instead of money. Ikari Buhin Inc., 5-22 Nishi Gotanda, Shinagawa-ku,

Tokyo 141 (03-490-1226), makes manually operated machines that sell cigarette lighters, sanitary napkins, shampoo, towels, and hotel sets (toothbrush, toothpaste, razor, comb).

page 86/Cross merchandising

Related to fusion business is the "rental window" concept. Businesses that don't need display windows rent them on a weekly and monthly basis. A tanning salon in Nishi Azabu, Tokyo (a trendy, affluent section), rents out its window on the condition that the display contain only stylish or healthy things. So far clients have been furniture and clothing importers. For information, contact Studio 82° F, Sanbu Building 1F, 1-12-5 Nishi Azabu, Minato-ku, Tokyo (03-405-1407).

page 87/Food and crop futures

If you buy a turkey, the farmer will send you periodic reports on how it's doing. Should it die before it is slaughtered for eating, you get a complete refund. For more information contact Shichimencho Shiiku Kumiai Owner-gakari (that is, the Association of Turkey Breeders) in Hokkaido at 0158-29-2111. You can buy a plot of trees from the forestry agency for ¥500,000. In twenty to thirty years you share in the profits at harvest. While you wait, you get discounts on lodgings at 190 places around the country, including 52 ski resorts. Loans are available. Contact 03-502-8111. Similarly, ¥200,000

buys you a stand of about eighty pine trees in Hokkaido. After twenty years, considering inflation and growth, you will make a profit of about 500 percent. You also receive a certificate declaring you a "special village person," and every year you are sent two or three items of food from the region your trees are located (organic ham, sausage, cheese, or mushrooms). Plus, you get discounts at ski and sports facilities and at local inns. Grandparents often buy these investments for their grandchildren. Contact Yakuba Sangyoka Furusato-gakari, Higashi Mokin-mura, Abashiri-gun, Hokkaido 099 (0152-66-2131). Joint venture ownership in cows, wild pigs, shrimp, pearl oysters, mushrooms, and persimmons, pears, and other fruit trees is also available. *Furusato Otodoke Book*, which lists information about all such types of agribusiness ventures, is published by Nihonsha Inc., 2-2-8 Kudan-minami, Chiyoda-ku, Tokyo 102 (03-262-2100).

pages 88–89/Independent kingdoms

Most of Japan's growing assortment of "independent" nations have their own passports and currencies. They have now formed a union to help each other devise ways of exploiting the marketing opportunities their status presents. The success of this kind of promotion is underscored by Hoshinokuni's experience. The town's initial investment was a single banner, but all the attendant free publicity offered by the media is estimated to have been worth ¥1.3 billion. The guidebook offers tips on how to enjoy the country. If you buy a passport, stores will stamp it with a "visa" when you make a purchase. A stamp qualifies you as a sweepstakes entrant. Addresses of the countries mentioned are as follows: (a) Hoshinokuni, c/o Seiwajisho, Nihon Seimei Yumeda Dai-ni Building, 3-24 Daiyuji-cho, Kita-ku, Osaka 530 (06-311-6631); (b) *Jipangu-koku,* Aizu, Ashinomaki-han, Ashinomaki Kanko Kyokai, Ashinomaki Oto-cho, Aizu Wakamatsu, Fukushima 969 (0242-92-2336); (c) Republic of Nikko Nikko, 1-16 Dake Onsen, Nihonmatsu, Fukushima 964 (0243-24-2310); (d) Survival Country, Akita Kaerumura, 25 Kariwano, Nishi Senboku-cho, Akita 014 (0187-75-2626); (e) Manga Kingdom, Hakuba Village Tourist Association, Hakuba, Nagano 399 (0261-72-3232).

page 90/Selected-item consumer days

For information about White Day, contact Zen Kashi Kyokai (the "All Sweet Association"), 5-12-4 Minami Aoyama, Minato-ku, Tokyo 107 (03-400-8901).

page 91/Convenient foodstuff packaging

Gift sets begin appearing on department store shelves in conjunction with major holidays and seasons, and are available for a wide variety of occasions, such as marriages, baby showers, housewarmings, school acceptance or graduation, getting a job, or just congratulations. The coffee set has four kinds of instant coffee blends, two kinds of nondairy creamers, two kinds of "special coffee sugar," all for about ¥5,000. For the same price you can get a pasta and spaghetti set instead, with three kinds of pasta, meat sauce, clam sauce, minestrone, olive oil, dried basil, and parmesan cheese. There is also the Häagen-Daz ice cream variety gift pack. A beer set offers different beers for the connoisseur. One gift set offers live shrimp. For more information contact Hankyu Department Store, 8-7 Tsunoda-cho Kita, Osaka 530 (06-361-1381).

pages 92—93/Novelty liquor, beer, and sake packaging

The sake maker Gekkeikan makes Hiya Can, which cools when shaken for those who like their sake chilled. Marketing tip: Kirin also offers a 350-milliliter can of beer packaged together with a small snack of dried cod, sea urchin, and nuts for ¥290.

page 94/Packaging of everyday products

For Toshiba batteries contact Toshiba Denchi Inc., 7-13-10 Ginza, Chuo-ku, Tokyo 104 (03-542-9171). The ice cream panties are called Candy Walk Panty

Stockings and are sold at the Fair Lady Fashion Lingerie boutique in Tokyo (03-346-2851).

page 96/Coordinated stationery systems

Modular paper systems offer a boon to graphic designers in the form of pre-printed, standard-sized boards for making mechanicals. These are sold in most art supply shops and represent a considerable savings over having to make up new boards for each job. *The Collections* is published by Nippon Shuppan Boeki, 1-2-1 Sarugaku-cho, Chiyoda-ku, Tokyo 101 (03-292-8541). Visual images here come from MOE, a monthly girls' magazine.

page 97/Generic merchandise store

Mujirushi Ryohin loosely means "No-Name Good Stuff." The stores sell only generic goods, although some department stores have Mujirushi Ryohin boutique corners with limited selections of merchandise. Clever merchandising throughout coordinates store decor, packaging, and fabric materials to a single austere aesthetic, which stresses simplicity and refinement as opposed to cheap and clunky. Product designers use ordinary materials in unfamiliar ways, such as plain corrugated cardboard wrappers to hold products, which effectively elevates a workhorse material into a design opportunity. All goods go with

all other goods: shirts, ties, and handkerchiefs go with your umbrella, your bicycle, and your backpack. Products change according to the season and to what the company sees as evolving consumer needs. There are never sales or discounts. The main store is at 5-50-6 Jingumae, Shibuya-ku, Tokyo 150 (03-407-7617).

pages 98–99/Prepaid designer telephone cards

If the phone companies in the United States can ever get card phones to proliferate and at the same time bring themselves to open up the business to outside entrepreneurs, the same phenomenon could easily happen in America. Potential profits are huge. Some cards in Japan have sold for as much as ¥500,000. The card collectors' book, called *Telecalle*, sells for ¥480 an issue and contains stories about popular cards, mythical cards, and idol cards, tips for collecting, retrospectives of great cards from previous years, interviews with telephone card personalities, speculations on the future of card trends, buy/sell columns, updates on prices, and so on. It is published by Orange Shuppan Inc., 505 Akasaka Barieru Maison, 3-16-5 Akasaka, Minato-ku, Tokyo 107 (03-583-0300). Cards are also being used for train fares and highway tolls. In a recent marketing twist, combo cards offer a train ticket, for example, tied to a commemorative telephone card. The Enoshima Electric Railway did this recently for its 85th anniversary (contact 0466-24-2713).

page 100/All-oracle building

Contact Uranaiyakata "Parimu," Sanzu Building B1, 1-7 Jingumae, Shibuya-ku, Tokyo 150 (03-497-5825).

page 101/Country bumpkin tours

More benign vacations offer a similar package to young women from the less-up-to-date provinces. With the tour comes hairstyling, makeup, and dress advice and rental, plus dinner at a fancy restaurant and a night in a glamorous Tokyo hotel. A once-in-a-lifetime opportunity to sample the kind of life seen only in magazines and movies.

pages 102–3/Love hotels

The premier love hotel in Japan is the Hotel Meguro Emperor, 2-1-6 Shimo-meguro, Meguro-ku, Tokyo 153 (03-494-1211).

pages 104–5/Theme weddings

The actual wedding ceremony is performed either at a Shinto shrine or Christian church, both of which may exist primarily for holding marriages or as part of a larger wedding complex. A sit-down, catered reception follows, with speeches and toasts by relatives and coworkers. Wedding agencies offer numerous services. On laser disk they have a catalog of all available wedding salons, hotels, party facilities, and catered food arrangements for the customer to choose from. They will also select gifts for the guests, make videos of the wedding and reception, put together a wedding photo album, decorate the interior of a new home, arrange for insurance, and obtain passports and visas for the honeymoon. Typically, a Japanese wedding ceremony and reception lasts two hours, has seventy guests, and costs almost ¥3 million. Tokyo Produce Konrei Center, Gomeikan Building 2F, 3-3-9 Shinjuku, Shinjuku-ku, Tokyo 160 (03-350-1512), is a total-planning wedding agency with twelve branches in Tokyo.

pages 106–7/Theme park concepts

Alternate name for the bike park is Cycle Paradise in Big Nature. A free shuttle bus connects it with the bullet train station twenty-five minutes away. Admission is ¥300. Ticket books are also available (¥1,700 for admission and six rides). Rides are cheap: The unusual bike square costs ¥300, the skyride ¥300, and the aerobic cycle ¥100. Contact Gunma Sports Cycle Center, Omineyama, Nii-haru-mura, Tone-gun, Gunma 379 (0278-64-1811). The maze concept was brought to Japan from New Zealand by Stuart Landsborough. Admission is about ¥500 for children. Contact Fureai

Sports Daigo "Gran Maze," 19-6 Yamanoshita, Momoyama-cho, Fushimi-ku, Kyoto 612 (075-621-2207).

pages 108—9/Hot springs attractions

The Arita Kanko Hotel, Yabitsu Kaigan, Arita, Wakayama 649 (0737-82-5201). For the bathing bears, contact Mr. Umezu at Takaragawa Osenkaku Ryokan, Onsen "Osenkaku," 1899 Oaza Fujiwara, Mina-kami-cho, Tone-gun, Gunma 379 (0278-75-2121). Rates for one person (two meals, room, unlimited bathing, tax, service) are ¥15,000–20,000 in the low season, ¥20,000 and up in the high season. For the monkey bath, contact Mr. Fujisue at Korakukan Ryokan, Jigoku-dani Onsen, Yamanouchi-cho, Shimotakai-gun, Nagano 381 (0269-33-4376). Price of ¥8,000 includes two meals, room, bathing, tax, and service. For the bath in the ice lake, contact Ryuichiro Sakino, who invented the idea, at Shikaribetsu Kohan Onsen, Shikaribetsu Kohan, Shikaoi-cho, Kato-gun, Hokkaido 081 (01566-7-2211). Made out of red pine, the tub is 2½ feet deep, 6 feet wide, and 8 feet long. A 500-foot hose brings 160° F water in from a near-by hot spring.

pages 110—11/Japanese inns

A day or two spent in a Japanese inn could teach most American and European hoteliers virtually all they need to know about service and about making guests feel as if they matter. In Japan, the notion of "honored guest" (okyaku-san) is still very much alive, and no-where is it more visible than at the Japanese inn. And . . . no tipping!

pages 112—13/Ultra-persistent video hard sell

ABC Camera, Kita Senri Branch, Fumedai, Suita, Osaka 565 (06-872-4309).

pages 114—15/Department store merchandising tips

Japanese department stores are aggressive information-age marketers. While their emphasis used to be mostly on quality, now they push taste, a reflection of how the Japanese have matured from buyers of necessities to a wealthy consumer class that can afford just about anything available in the world markets. Merchandising now emphasizes lifestyle concepts. Most stores have so-called culture zones, event spaces, hobby centers, and sports plazas. They also offer a variety of amenities and services that make them a pleasure to shop in. Courteous and knowledgeable personnel who care—or appear to care—about customer satisfaction are the most visible manifestation of high-quality service. Little things like disposable plastic umbrella covers given out at entrances to eliminate mess on floors and clothing enhance this feeling. Food

APPENDIX

floors (usually in basements) offer free samples of exotic and cooked foods. Kids can spend time at video theaters while their parents shop. Other amenities for children include supervised playrooms for toddlers, diaper-changing areas, children's dentists, and even consultants on child behavior. Employees at one store wear day-glo yellow shirts for easy identification. Upscale stores have art exhibits and galleries that buy and sell original works by well-known artists. Stores also offer classes in traditional arts and crafts (like flower arranging) and computer programming.

pages 116–17/Concept buildings

Seed, Spiral, and Wave are all part of the Seibu group, which among other things also owns a baseball team and stadium, an amusement park, and a huge department store, not to mention the train line that takes people to all these places. The Seed Building concept refers to "seed of new department store life." Here is a brief rundown of its contents by floor (floors, names, and sales concepts change periodically). *B2*: The Wave, selling sound and video and information. *B1*: The Microbeam, a back alley dispensing street fashion and culture. Staff here don't try to help you find things, so as to promote the joy of rummaging. *1*: The Seed Gate, that is, the entry level, where people can gather, hang out, leave messages for each other on a com-

puter system, drink at a bar, or view the promotion spaces rented out to other companies on a weekly basis. *2*: Express, where international fashion is the theme and the excitement and glamour of the New York, Milan, London, and Paris circuit are recreated. *3*: Season, which evokes the time of the year with seasonal merchandise and an elaborate stage-set atmosphere. *4*: The Parts, where clothing is sold separately and is not coordinated by style or by designer. Mix and match for adventurous Tokyo dressers. *5*: The Closet, a center for old durables, the nontrendy items that will never go out of fashion. Samples are displayed, and all merchandise is sold in sealed packages. Customers move about the aisles with shopping carts and pay at a register as if in a supermarket. *6*: The Party has theme boutiques, party wear, casual wear (the idea is that a party "can just be two people"). The pitch here appeals to the lure of the nighttime and the snobbism of the city. Staff offer lots of advice and will coordinate and plan your parties for you. They also custom make uniforms (using any designer whose works are sold at Seed), and design stationery and office supplies. *7*: The Office offers comfortable clothes for work and daytime wear. *8*: The Next sells "the force of creativity" and has the feeling of a studio. Lots of trendy designers' clothes, with the exhibiting spaces changing frequently. *9*: The Relation, which has the feeling of a museum with quality merchandise by a few well-established designers like Issey Miyake. Also located here is a tearoom and cafeteria. *10*: Seed Hall, where the philosophy of the building is manifested in art at a high-tech multipurpose space for exhibitions, cinema, and performances. The idea of the Spiral Building is based not simply on the structure of the building but on a metaphysical notion of spirals. The top floors of Wave contain a recording studio and state-of-the-art computer graphics studio. Wave's rear entrance features a holographic Buddhist shrine. Contact Seibu Department Stores, Sunshine 60, 3-1-1 Higashi Ikebukuro, Toshima-ku, Tokyo 170 (03-989-0111). Among the courses offered at Tokyu Hands are stained glass and pottery making, weaving, decoupage, patchwork, silkscreening, bookmaking, glass blowing, jewelry making, leather work, rattan, woodworking, yarn spinning, and enameling. One-day classes are also offered each month. If a purchase exceeds ¥3,000, delivery is free (most department stores in Japan offer free delivery, usually within a day or two by special courier). Instant loans are available with just an ID card.

page 120/Change machines and real-time maps

For information on bus locators, contact Toei Bus, Kotsu Kaikan Building, 2-10-1 Yurakucho, Chiyoda-ku, Tokyo 100. Change machines cost ¥650,000–800,000, or ¥1 million for those that read magnetic strips. They are made by NEC Home Electronics Inc., Sumitomo Mita Building, 5-37-8 Shiba, Minato-ku, Tokyo 108 (03-454-3637).

page 121/Public pollution monitors

For further information, contact Tokyo-to Kankyo Hozon Kyoku, 1-7-1 Yurakucho, Chiyoda-ku, 100 (03-214-7411).

page 122/Building conventions

For information on building wraps, contact Tokyo City Development Department, 3-5-1 Marunouchi, Chiyoda-ku, Tokyo 100 (03-212-5111, ext. 25468).

page 123/Video billboards on wheels

Currently seven Mobotrons serve Tokyo. For information about rental, contact Topgun Co., Akasaka Lion Building 8F, 1-1-2 Motoakasaka, Minato-ku, Tokyo 107 (03-478-7001). Purchase price of a Mobotron is ¥70 million. Another, more low-budget solution is offered by Apple Board Co. A procession of ten red 50cc motorscooters (which by Japanese law cannot travel faster than 20 mph) driven by ten attractive young women (to attract attention, says the company president) travel along the shoulders of roads around town, each carrying the same advertising sign. Very visible and effective. Cost is ¥3 million for eight hours each day for six days.

pages 124–25/Unique TV shows

An experimental prime-time sitcom called "There Is No Night That Man Doesn't Cry" mixes many forms of contemporary TV into one. The gags revolve around an ad agency, but interspersed are all kinds of real life information. Titles of background music are displayed on the screen, movie reviews are injected into bar scenes (with clips from the films), authors playing cameo roles suddenly take out their recent books and display them for the camera. One segment called "Extra Present of the Show" was a two-minute scene showing three admen admiring the underarms of a porno actress known for her hairiness. Many Japanese TV shows are still broadcast live.

page 126/Effective TV commercials

It is common knowledge that many big-name American stars lend their celebrity to products and commercials in Japan that they would be embarrassed to be associated with in their own country. Woody Allen appeared in ads for a department store. George Lucas hawks electronics goods for Matsushita. Paul Newman endorses coffee and credit cards. Sometimes the payoff for these celebrities is in increased celebrity. Kathleen Battle, the opera singer, was unknown in Japan before her Nikka Whiskey TV commercials—and she then sold out her 1987 Japan concert tour. Among the perennial favorites in Japan are Olivia Hussey, James Coburn, and, until his death, Orson Welles. The largest Japanese advertising agency, often involved in setting up celebrity deals, is Dentsu Inc., 1-11-10 Tsukiji, Chuo-ku, Tokyo 104 (03-544-5111).

page 127/Bus and subway advertising

Some buses also display a digital readout that, for an extra fee, gives the name of the announced store and its phone number. For information, call Kokusai Hiyoshiki (03-984-5551). Ad prices in subways are reasonable, considering that almost thirty million people live in the Tokyo area, many of them regular subway riders. Prices vary according to ridership. On the crowded Hibiya Line, for example, side wall posters cost ¥778,000 a month for 340 of them. You can hang 1,050 posters for two days for ¥660,000. Prices do not include the costs of manufacturing and printing the posters. Contact Taito Kosokudo Kotsukaidan, 3-19-6 Higashi Ueno, Taito-ku, Tokyo 110 (03-832-2111).

page 128/Tissue paper giveaways

One company that provides tissue packets is Chigiwa Insatsu, 2-25-3 Tori-cho, Minami-ku, Yokohama, Kanagawa 231 (045-731-0079). Standard minimum order is 10,000 units, with two-color printing on a paper insert. For jobs over 100,000 units, the company will print on the plastic wrapper as well.

page 129/Transferable debt payments

For information contact Zenkoku Ginko Kyokai Rengokai, Tokyo Ginko Kyokai, 1-3-1 Marunouchi, Chiyoda-ku, Tokyo 100 (03-216-3761).

pages 130–31/Corporate comic books

One of the leading creators of corporate comic books is Business Comic-sha Inc. in Tokyo. After an initial meeting with the client to discuss needs, the company provides rough sketches. The client can back out at this point with no charge. If the proposal is accepted, Business Comic-sha will produce a fifty- to sixty-page comic in two to three months. The company uses freelance artists and holds all copyrights to prevent the client from using characters and format again without paying an extra fee. Business Comic-sha is at 8-12-5-307 Nishi Gotanda, Shinagawa-ku, Tokyo 141 (03-492-0960).

pages 132–33/Magazine and comic book concepts

Introduction to the Japanese Economy was drawn by Shotaro Ishinomori, one of Japan's best-known comic book artists, known also for his samurai tales. The book became a national bestseller, at a third of the price of the weighty, "serious," all-text volume on which it was based (both the text and comic versions were published by Nihon Keizai Shinbunsha, publisher of Japan's equivalent of the *Wall Street Journal*). Other instructional comic books like the traffic law book are *Inheritance Made Easy* and *The Perfect Secretary* (explaining business etiquette). Some magazines have stores or grant licenses to stores that carry a range of merchandise displaying the magazine logo. *Mono* ("Things") is one. To entice browsers, some magazines leave the first ten pages open and seal the rest in plastic that can only be removed after purchase.

pages 134–35/Unique book concepts

Along the lines of the "everybody poops" book is *Onara wa Roka no Keihoki*, or "Farts Are a Warning Sign of Getting Old." The book says that it is unhealthy to restrain yourself, that loudness is a sign of healthy intestines, and that the strong, silent types indicate poor digestion. Another popular book concept involves blood types. People are grouped according to A, B, AB, and O. Most Japanese are type A (said to favor group activity), while most Americans are O (sign of a pioneer spirit). Among the types of bookstores found in Japan are those that sell only mail-order catalogs from around the world.

page 136/Teaching basic values

Many schools have supplemental programs that encourage children to go out and interact in the community. Children visit nursing schools to help care for babies, go to rest homes to cheer up senior citizens, or venture out onto the streets of the town to clean up litter. For more information on schools, contact Mr. Yokota at Shinagawa-ku Kyoiku Iinkai Shidoshitsu, 1-28-3 Nishi Shinagawa, Shinagawa-ku, Tokyo 141 (03-787-1161, ext. 464).

page 137/Preventing auto accidents

For convex mirrors, contact Meguro Kotsuanzenka Doboku-bu, c/o Meguro Ward Hall, 2-4-5 Chuo-cho, Meguro-ku, Tokyo 152 (03-715-1111). Until the mid-1970s, the policeman figures were sculpted and made of plastic, but vengeful citizens kept cutting their heads off. The metal ones now used are cheaper, more durable, and movable. Each costs ¥20,000. They are also used at banks to deter robberies. While everyone knows they're phony, they give the impression of a strong police presence, and also help confuse people as to where the true police are. They don't need bullet-proof vests either. For information, contact San S Giken Inc., Odakyu Nishi Shinjuku Building 4F, 1-47-1 Hatsudai, Shibuya-ku, Tokyo 151 (03-375-1811), which develops products for Japanese police departments.

page 138/Police boxes

Most police boxes are rather non-descript structures. Often they are designed into buildings, stations, and pedestrian walkways rather than standing outside on the curb. On one main intersection in Ginza, however, a two-story "designer" *koban* by architect Kazumasa Yamashita has a copper peaked roof and red and brown striped walls. American and European police authorities have been aware of the *koban* system for years and are devising ways of adopting it in their own cities.

page 140/Telephone aids for the disabled

One very nice thing about the "do-me-a-favor" book is that people who are approached with it on the street know that they are not about to be asked for small change. All phone services mentioned are available from NTT, 1-4-30 Roppongi, Minato-ku, Tokyo 106 (03-585-7160).

page 141/Making cities safer for the blind

The textured pavements are called Yudo Blocks ("Leading Blocks") and were developed and manufactured by Anzen Kotsu Shiken Kenkyu Center, Sumitomo Seimei Building 17F, 1-1-1 Yangai-machi, Okayama City, Okayama 700 (0862-23-1711). For information about aids to the blind, contact Nippon Mojin Shokuno Kaihatsu Center (that is, the Japan Center for Developing Skills of the Blind), 10-3 Honshio-cho, Shinjuku-ku, Tokyo 160 (03-341-0900). Newly designed paper money in Japan is embossed with small dots that enable the blind to distinguish between the various denominations.

pages 142–43/Message and information centers

Another kind of electronic billboard sponsored by the retail merchants association is the guide computer. Located on almost every block in shopping and entertainment districts, the computer offers up-to-date information on restaurants, clothing stores, events, and bargain sales. When the menu for bars is selected, for example, the computer displays options for price, type of mood, style of drinks, and accompanying food. After the next selection, the information requested appears on the screen with a map and a few other alternatives in case the place you want is closed that day. Many guide computers also have a miniprinter that provides a permanent record of the information displayed: good for when you set off into the jumble of Japanese streets.

pages 144–45/Magazine House

Magazine House, 3-13-10 Ginza, Chuo-ku, Tokyo 104 (03-545-7111).

page 146/Public gathering places

Sony Plaza is at 5-3-1 Ginza, Chuo-ku, Tokyo 104 (03-573-2371), just down the road from Yurakucho Station and above the subway station where the Hibiya and Ginza lines meet. You can ride to the top and then spiral down the inside as you go from shop to shop, each one a short flight of steps down from the one before.

page 147/Taking corporate responsibility

Japan is much less litigious than the United States, where admission of responsibility at any point can set off a flurry of lawsuits and liability payments. Also, employees in Japan both think of themselves and are perceived as part of a monolithic corporate group. Strong group consciousness in Japan makes it easier for all blame to be shifted around and focused on an individual at the top. Often the president is sacrificed in order to protect the organization. For information on the Japan Air Lines incidents, contact Mr. Nishihara of JAL at 2-7-3 Marunouchi, Chiyoda-ku, Tokyo 100 (03-284-2106).

page 149/Encouraging employee creativity

Prizes awarded at the All-Honda contest include the Mechanical Prize (for technical excellence), the Dream Prize (for advanced, futuristic design), the Nice Idea Prize (for most convenient), and the Unique Prize (for most strange and surprising). The spectators select the Golden Icon Prize for the most popular project, "icon" being short for "idea contest." For information, contact Mr. Wakao, Honda Giken Kogyo, 2-1-1 Minami Aoyama, Minato-ku, Tokyo 107 (03-423-1111).

THANKS

Sampei Abe, Alfred Birnbaum, Steve Bisset, Dave Bong, Nick Bornoff, Sloan Carr, Shi Yu Chen, Kit Cherry, Judith Connor, Alan Gleason, Hiroko Hanai, Keiko Hirayama, Hiroko Horiguchi, Andrew S. Howell, Tom Ingalls, John Ingham, Sunao Ishii, Michael Jamentz, Emiko Kaji, Lucy Seligman Kanazawa, Michiyo Kashiwagi, Sam Kawakami, Naoko Kawamura, Jan Kawata, Mari Kida, Jonathan Lloyd-Owen, Sarah J. Lonsdale, Daniel Masler, Ray Miles, Akihiko Morishita, Yoichi Muragaki, Kazuko Murono, Megumi Nakatani, James J. Nelson, Kunio Nishimura, Kumi Ohta, Kazuko Okuma, Setsuko Okura, Taki Ono, Don Philippi, Peter Popham, Erik Schmid, Mark Schreiber, Dave Spector, Takayama Architects & Assoc., Naoko Terazaki, Kyoichi Tsuzuki, Charles T. Whipple, Tamotsu Yagi, Teruhiko Yumura.

SPECIAL THANKS

The Kato Family—Hisako, Kuniko, Taku, and Yoichi for loving support while working on this project. **Flamingo Studio**—for introducing us to illustrator Shack Mihara. **Michael Phillips**—for his inspiration. **Frederik Schodt**—for an abundance of good ideas and optimism. **Alexander Besher**—for help and encouragement. **Japan Free Press**—"a digest of the Japanese mass media," a publication chock full of good ideas. **Bill Womack**—for help and advice on art direction and design. **Peter Goodman**—for co-developing the concept of this book.